MOONLIGHTING FOR FUN AND PROFIT

Keep Your Day Job While Earning Extra Income

ROBERT E. MITCHELL

A CITADEL PRESS BOOK
Published by Carol Publishing Group

A Citadel Press Book
Published by Carol Publishing Group
Citadel Press is a registered trademark of Carol Communications, Inc.

Editorial, sales and distribution, rights and permissions inquiries should be addressed to Carol Publishing Group, 120 Enterprise Avenue, Secaucus, N.J. 07094.

In Canada: Canadian Manda Group, One Atlantic Avenue, Suite 105, Toronto, Ontario M6K 3E7

Carol Publishing Group books may be purchased in bulk at special discounts for sales promotion, fund-raising, or educational purposes. Special editions can be created to specifications. For details, contact Special Sales Department, Carol Publishing Group, 120 Enterprise Avenue, Secaucus, N.J. 07094.

Manufactured in the United States of America

10 9 8 7 6 5 4 3 2 1

Library of Congress Cataloging-in-Publication Data

Mitchell, Robert, 1959–
    Moonlighting for fun and profit : keep your day job while earning extra income / Robert E. Mitchell.
        p. cm.
    Includes index.
    ISBN 0–8065–1987–8 (pb)
    1. Supplementary employment—United States. I. Title.
HD5854.55.U5M58 1998
331.25'72—dc21   98–4972
                                                      CIP

CONTENTS

ACKNOWLEDGMENTS

No author writes a book entirely by himself or herself, and *Moonlighting for Fun and Profit* is no exception. Chief among those who helped create the book are:

Sydney Fox, who lent her expertise as a financial planner at WestAmerica, an investment firm in Scottsdale, Arizona, to the chapter about budgeting income; Rachael Thomas, an activities therapist at a New York City hospital who shared with us her experience in the part-time work world to write about how to turn part-time employment into full-time work; Susanna Daniel, a recent graduate of Columbia University who until landing a full-time marketing position at a New York City news media firm has held many part-time jobs; and Afarin Majidi, who during her days juggling part-time jobs became an expert on stress management before obtaining a full-time job at *Departures* magazine, where she is an editorial staff member.

In addition, I want to express my gratitude to my editor Monica Harris and my agent Jeremy Solomon. Their hard work on the book's behalf has been invaluable.

INTRODUCTION

Nearly eight million Americans—from almost every background imaginable—are enjoying the rewards and joys of having a second job. There are actors auditioning for acting jobs during the day and waiting tables at night. There are men and women who are accountants, retailers, and haircutters during the day, but who work as musicians, copy editors, and bartenders at night. And there are those who teach high school during the day—me—but who've worked in bookstores, taught night-school courses, and worked as messengers during the evenings. The variety of part-time employment is nearly as varied as the constellations in the sky, and the individuals who have part-time jobs are equally as varied. Here is how the *Wall Street Journal* recently described the country's part-time work force: "Most part-timers are voluntary. [In 1996] 76.6 percent of those with part-time jobs said they didn't want full-time work. Among them are students needing extra cash, older workers who don't want or can't afford full retirement, parents with children but no child care and people choosing part-time work for lifestyle reasons—essentially college-educated professionals who prefer to spend more time at home and at play."

Moonlighting for Fun and Profit is a must-read for anyone contemplating seeking a second job. No other book offers you so much advice and information on how to find the second job that is best suited to your needs, interests, and goals. *Moonlighting for Fun and Profit* will tell you how to use the Internet effectively to seek a part-time job, and it will tell you how and when to use temp agencies in your job search. But finding the perfect part-time job is only part of what *Moonlighting for Fun and Profit* offers. The book also gives you tips on how to balance your life—socially and financially—once you've obtained that second job. How, for example, will you keep up with friends once you've gotten a second job? How can you remain professionally reliable with two jobs? How will you budget and invest your newly acquired income? You will find that these and other essential questions will be answered in these pages in a format that is accessible and helpful.

Moonlighting for Fun and Profit wasn't written by academics in an ivory tower, or by people who have never held down two jobs at once. *Moonlighting for Fun and Profit* was written by those who know best: men and women who, from personal experiences, know the rewards and challenges of part-time employment. The writers and researchers who compiled this book have worked part-time as messengers and in editorial offices. They've volunteered in local hospitals and soup kitchens. And they've temped as receptionists and research assistants at law firms and talent agencies. There is one common denominator that each writer and researcher in these pages shares, however: They've found part-time work to be rewarding for more than just financial reasons. They've also found part-time work to be deeply satisfying and gratifying.

In *Moonlighting for Fun and Profit* you'll read real-life stories about individuals who have found rewarding second jobs. For example, you'll read about an accountant who successfully sought a part-time position writing music. He didn't seek the job for money reasons, though. He sought the job as a creative alternative to a job he says left him feeling uninspired at the end of a day. "I couldn't leave my full-time job because of the income and benefits, but I knew I needed some way to keep up with my interests in music, so finding a job writing music for independent filmmakers was perfect," he says. As part of our research for the book, we also talked to a young woman who had just moved to a large city from college. "I didn't know anyone when I moved here," she says. "When I was in school I did a great deal of volunteer work at a soup kitchen, and I met many people that way. So I knew finding volunteer work in the city to which I had just moved would be a way to start making new friends. That's why I got my job working at the ASPCA [The American Society for the Prevention of Cruelty to Animals]. I've met several people at the society, and knowing them has helped make living in such a large city a bit easier."

For many of us, having a second job has meant obtaining a much-needed second income. Credit-card debt, mortgage payments, and college loans sometimes seem insurmountable without the income generated from part-time work to supplement our full-time jobs. Carl, a young man living on his own in Indianapolis, was overwhelmed by debt—he was barely keeping up with minimum payments on his credit-card bills. Carl, however, stumbled on a new opportunity waiting tables at one of his favorite restaurants. With his added income from the restaurant, Carl became credit-card-debt free. "The day I made my last payment to MasterCard was one of my happiest days ever," he said. "Ever since then I haven't felt as if someone is looking over my shoulder." We've included Carl's story—and a chapter on how to budget and invest your new income—in Moonlighting for Fun and Profit.

Finally, many individuals seek part-time work as a way to explore other career possibilities that might be developed into full-time work. For example, while teaching high school during the day, I worked part-time at a local bookstore during the evenings and on the weekends because I thought someday I would like to own a bookstore. What I learned is that there is a great deal more to owning a bookstore than just talking about the latest literary sensation and shelving books. In fact, those tasks are just a small part of the job; I learned that running a bookstore is a time-consuming and complicated endeavor—a lesson I could have fully appreciated only by having had that on-the-job, part-time experience.

In short, holding down a part-time job allows you the chance to find your dream job, whether it's one you're seeking for a creative outlet or for financial gain. When you're seeking part-time work—no matter what the reason—make certain it's one you find challenging and rewarding. Refer to the first chapter of *Moonlighting for Fun and Profit* for details on how to find such a position most effectively. Don't forget, however, that a second job isn't permanent. Always act professionally. You'll be amazed by the job connections you can make through part-time work. Also, you'll no doubt want to use a supervisor at your part-time job as a reference at some point in your professional career.

Holding down a second job is no easy task. Anyone who has ever done so can tell you that. As part of our research for *Moonlighting for Fun and Profit*, we talked with a thirty-two-year-old man who realized while he was at his part-time job that he needed to be at an appointment for his full-time employer. "It was a nightmare when I realized my mistake," he said. "I quickly called my boss, telling him about the situation and that it would never happen again. He said that he hoped it wouldn't. I was mortified." What our friend realized is that the key to maintaining two jobs successfully—and this should come as no surprise—is organization. Study after study shows that the more organized you are, the more successful you're going to be, personally and professionally. That's why we devote a significant section of *Moonlighting for Fun and Profit* to helping you develop effective organizational and time-management skills.

Many of America's full-time workers have sought part-time work for financial and personal reasons. In fact, the number that do so each year continues to rise. In 1980, for example, 4.9 percent of the workforce held more than one job. Today, that figure has risen to 6.2 percent.

Moonlighting for Fun and Profit will prove to be an indispensable tool as you begin your search for your ideal part-time job.

MOONLIGHTING
FOR FUN
AND PROFIT

◆ ◆ ◆

Broadening Horizons With Part-Time Work: Margie's Story

Margie is a thirty-eight-year-old aspiring actress. Having studied acting as both an undergraduate and graduate student, Margie left the world of academia prepared to embark on an exciting career in acting. As she soon learned, upon graduation, the glamour and glitter of Broadway and Hollywood were not so easy to come by. Though unwilling to give up her dream and forget all the years of hard work that went into training to become an actress, Margie had a difficult decision to make. Was she going to give up her dream and settle down with a job, or was she going to keep trying to make it as an actress, struggling as she had for so long?

"It was really hard for me to think that all that effort I had put into what I consider my art, what I love to do, was a big waste," she said. "Even today I can't give up the dream, and although the acting jobs I get are fewer and farther between as the years have passed, I won't give up. I just can't bear to do it, if for no other reason than that I think I'm good at it." But Margie realized that she had another option and did not have to choose between acting and a career. She was aware that taking a day job would make getting to auditions more difficult and that her work and acting schedules would overlap at periods in her life.

3

She was not prepared to continue waitressing as she had been doing for several years.

"As I began getting older, I started to see that maybe taking another career path wasn't such a bad idea. Before, I had been waiting tables, and that was fine for that period in my life, but I began to realize that I could do other things as well. I really wanted to try something new and maybe learn something, too." So, Margie began to look at her skills and education to evaluate her options and qualifications. "I had a degree in theater from a relatively prestigious college, and I figured that had to count for something! And I talked to a friend of mine who was working as an editor at a magazine and she suggested that I try to find work as a fact checker."

Margie didn't even know what a fact checker was, but she began asking questions and realized that she was well qualified for such work. She learned that publishing was a career that interested her. More important, she saw that her income from fact-checking could help pay the bills while giving her the flexibility of schedule she needed to continue her acting career. "Fact-checking is all about taking a manuscript and going over all the information to make sure that it's accurate," explained Margie. "It's far from glamorous, but it really beats waiting tables, especially since it's freelance work. I could work at different magazines and learn about how they work and what editors and writers actually do."

The work appealed to Margie's free spirit and gave her a unique freedom. "It's especially nice to freelance, because you don't end up doing the same thing and going to the same office day in, day out. The work varies from job to job, magazine to magazine." Although the work was unsteady at first, Margie built up a list of different editors for whom she has worked on a regular basis. The jobs now keep rolling in. "I actually have to turn down many jobs because my schedules overlap, unless I can do the work at home. There are hardly any periods in which I have little or no work."

Having worked as a fact checker for so many years has also granted her a sense of freedom and choice. "Some magazines allow me to take the manuscripts home, while others require that I do it in the office. It's really just policy, and it depends on the publication." Asked which she prefers, she says, "Oh, working at home, for sure. There's no better way to have to do work, unless I'm acting or auditioning, of course. When I don't have to be in the office from nine to five, my days are free, which is convenient, so I don't have to worry about being late for a tryout or audition. I can leave time to go to my theater group and do my fact-checking work around my other priorities."

Working in publishing has also had the added benefit of expanding her professional options. "At first, interviewing for fact-checking jobs took time away from my auditions, which was discouraging. Going into the publishing offices, first as an interviewee, then as a part-time employee, allowed me to see the publishing industry in a realistic way. I saw writers and editors who were just like me. I mean, they didn't seem any brighter or more creative than me. To be honest, as a kid I had wanted to be a writer, but acting became more of an interest. At one of the magazines I was doing some work for, I had a story idea that I thought would be perfect for their publication. One day I went to an editor at the magazine and pitched the idea, which was a theater review. He thought it was a good idea, and he told me to go for it. I did, he liked what he read, and I've been doing short pieces for the magazine ever since."

Margie feels that with her part-time job she's able to use her creative skills as an actress and writer to the fullest extent. "I'm still going to auditions," she said. "I don't think I'll ever stop doing that. I'm also really enjoying my work as a writer and fact checker. The work has added a new dimension to my life, one that has broadened my interests and areas of expertise. But acting is still my priority, so I'll keep on with my magazine work until I get that leading role on Broadway."

about who you really are and asks you to look both at your abilities and at your limits. In a way, it's asking you to look at yourself the way others see you.

To start, ask yourself the following questions, and answer them not just to yourself but on paper. Writing is thinking on paper, and having the chance to see your answers in such a way will help you to understand yourself better. Also, it's important to get input from family and friends. Inform them that you're thinking of getting a second job and ask them what they think your strengths and weaknesses are. Listen carefully to their answers as you may learn something new about yourself that you didn't already know before. And don't be afraid to take constructive criticism. If the people you're talking to really care about you, they're only trying to help.

What kind of time commitment can I afford? Picture yourself working three-shift weekends. Or weeknights, after getting home from your day job. Or summers, when you might otherwise be lazing on a beach or traveling. Think realistically about your present-time commitments and how much time you have free. "Free time" is relative. You can redistribute the time you *waste*, but can you sacrifice the time you spend relaxing and socializing? The amount of time you are willing to commit to a part-time job may depend on how you spend your time presently, or on how much extra income you need. A part-time job doesn't need to be easy or convenient, but it should be realistic. And it should add more to your life than it takes away.

For example, look at your present daily schedule. Determine how many hours you spend working, relaxing, and running errands. In what ways can you rearrange your schedule? Can you save your errands for the weekend to make room for a part-time job on weekday nights? Can you wake up earlier? After you have rearranged your schedule, how many hours are free? Can you devote this time to a new job?

How much extra income do I want? How much do I need? Salaries for part-time jobs range as fully as those for full-time jobs. Freelancing and consulting can be quite profitable. For example, many copy editors and fact checkers earn $30 an hour. Bookkeepers make $35–40 an hour, and computer programmers can make as much as $50. Temporary work can be a steady source of solid income if you develop a relationship with the right employment agency. Volunteering has its nonfinancial perks—it can be a great way to meet people, and it can offer personal satisfaction many full-time careers cannot. Volunteering can also offer you needed work experience and future job contacts. Think about your current income, your desired (but realistic) lifestyle and budget, and the discrepancy between the two. Ask yourself exactly how much more money you need. Chances are, if you have decided to take a part-time job for financial reasons, you have already given thought to these pertinent issues.

When considering part-time employment, be certain to find out how much the position pays. Also, ask the employer about the company's pay schedule. Will you get paid once a month or weekly? If you're going for a part-time job because you're seeking much-needed financial help, answers to such questions will be important.

What sort of job would I settle for? Is this a move I would make only if it was perfect? If your primary motive is the experience of having a different job, you will want to wait for a position that fulfills your part-time job dreams. Since you already have a full-time job, you might want to work part-time at something you are interested in or fascinated by, something you have always wanted to explore but have been too practical to try. For example, if you have always wanted to own a bookstore, try working in one part-time. This way you can get a practical sense of the day-to-day details of bookstore retail, as well as fulfill a fantasy. If you are cash-driven, you might want to think about how little money you are willing to take, and hold out for at least that amount. Also, once you accept a part-time job, you won't find the time to keep looking for other part-time work. Be certain you're satisfied with your new position financially before signing any papers.

What are my strengths? Weaknesses? Skills? How can these strengths and skills translate into a job? Even if your goal is to have a completely original part-time job, different from your full-time work in every way, you would be surprised how flexible your skills can be, and in how many environments they are useful. For example, someone who works in public relations might be a valuable bookstore employee because of her ability to speak to customers about a product. Or, a bookkeeper at a law firm might take part-time work handling the accounting for a museum or nonprofit group. If you speak another language, you could translate part-time, or tutor. If you're a recreational aerobics fanatic, take some time to get the necessary credentials, then teach an aerobics class or two, or become a professional trainer. All sorts of people, with all sorts of skills (and lack thereof), work at part-time jobs.

As an exercise, take a moment to write down the following:

Your artistic, analytical, and business skills
Your experience
Your talents and hobbies
Your personality traits

Any combination of these might translate into interesting and rewarding part-time work. The following is an example of this type of brainstorming.

Skills	*Possibilities*
Computer skills, including Macintosh and IBM experience, Microsoft Word, Excel and Photoshop.	Dictation work and practically any office work available.
General office skills—e.g., faxing, typing (50 wpm), making travel arrangements, light bookkeeping, filing, scheduling appointments, etc.	Office work as a receptionist, secretary, or office manager. General office skills prepare you for anything.

Experience

Four years working as a receptionist in a doctor's office. Answered phones, dealt with patients, maintained doctor's schedule.	Night-shift work answering phones. Personal secretary to an executive.
Two years as an au pair for two children, ages nine and twelve. Light cooking and cleaning included.	Childcare work as a nanny or baby-sitter; perhaps even in a day-care center.
Three years on the high-school soccer team.	The local community center or YMCA for coaching or assistant coaching.

Free-associate and brainstorm part-time job ideas. See what you come up with when you think about how your hobbies translate into work. For example, could you teach a pottery class at the local YMCA? Could you tutor high-school students in French? Think about the flexibility of your present job. If you wanted to leave every Thursday at 3:00 P.M. to teach an arts-and-crafts class at a local community center, would your boss let you make up the time in the evening or on the weekend? Brainstorming involves thinking about prospects from every angle—every part of your life, from family connections to local businesses to friends.

Evaluate your options, needs, and wants. Think of your ideal part-time job. What does it pay? What are the hours? Think of the most nightmarish part-time job possible. What are its wages and hours? Most likely, your part-time job will be a cross between the two, more closely resembling the former. Think about what you are missing in your full-time work. Is it money? Prestige? Creative opportunity? Community? Think about what type of part-time work would satisfy what is lacking in your full-time work, and prioritize those qualities. Which job quality is imperative, and which can you live without? If you are most in need of money, your part-time job should probably focus on steady, medium- to high-paying temporary work. If you are bored with your current environment and money is not an issue, you might think about working somewhere you enjoy visiting, like a local cafe or bookstore, or volunteering at a lively nonprofit organization.

How's your health? The impact of seeking and obtaining part-time employment will have on you physically and emotionally cannot be overstated. Many people take on a second job without considering what the impact of having the added time commitment and responsibilities will have on them. When thinking about getting a second job, ask yourself these questions: How much time can you afford physically on the job? Will working more than forty hours a week be overly stressful on you emotionally? Some people, especially younger ones just out of college, are often capable of working more hours than someone, say, in her fifties. Or the younger person might be able to take on more physically demanding work. That may be an overstatement, however, as many people in their fifties and older work a number of jobs to make ends meet or for personal satisfaction. The point is, no matter what your age, you must evaluate your physical and emotional capabilities before seeking additional employment.

THE JOB HUNT IS ON

After evaluating your part-time career goals, it is time to begin the search. But before exploring the infinite possibilities outside your personal world, consider the aspects of the process that you can control. This will be quick and painless for some, and long and arduous for others. Prepare to settle into the hunt. Think of the process as a challenge—one that will eventually reap many personal and professional rewards.

PERSONAL RESOURCES

Make a list of friends, family, and acquaintances you consider possible resources. These are often people who are in positions to hire, people who intimately know a business that interests you, or people who have jobs and lifestyles you admire. Maybe they could give you a few clues about how to get where you want.

Also, think about the places you visit and enjoy in your everyday life. An investment banker might find that working at his favorite bookstore quells his need for a different environment; a teacher might enjoy a summer job waiting tables at her favorite cafe; a librarian might work nights as a bartender in a local bar; a bookkeeper might work a few hours a week instructing a yoga class at her local gym. Spend a few days evaluating every place you go for its employment potential. For example, think about who you would approach for a receptionist position at your health club, or for a waiter staff position at your favorite restaurant. Have you ever talked to the manager? Would she recognize you? Be friendly. Businesses often hire friends and regular customers.

YOUR RESUMÉ

The importance of the resumé can never be over-emphasized. Have three, four, or ten people you trust review and critique your resumé before you distribute it. In a nutshell, your resumé should be one page, precise, and professional looking. Writing your resumé is like writing a newspaper article about yourself. Your resumé is uniquely *you*. Take the time to make sure it is as complete and to the point as possible.

Here are a few tips for your resumé:

- It should be typed or done on a word processor.
- It should not be longer than a single page, especially because you're seeking part-time employment.
- It should be written on plain white paper, preferably paper that is of high quality.
- Your name, address, and phone number should be written clearly at the top of your resumé.

- Avoid fancy type or design on your resumé, unless, perhaps, you're going for a position at an art store or design shop.

Additionally, considering that your goal is to find a *part-time* job, your resumé, and the accompanying cover letter, should reflect those specific needs. One possibility is to include an *objective* or *statement of purpose* at the beginning of the document, detailing your needs and availability, and possibly even your reason for seeking part-time work. Here is an example of the objective portion of a part-time job seeker's resumé:

OBJECTIVE

To utilize my skills and experience in a supplemental employment experience; to work weekends between the hours of 8:00 A.M. and midnight, or weekdays after 5:00 P.M.

Additionally, your resumé should include the following:

Personal information   This includes your name, address, telephone number, and, if available, e-mail address.

Work experience   Here you will want to list all the jobs you have had, starting with your present and recent employment. Each listing should include the name and address of the employer and the time period of each employment. State clearly the nature of your duties for each job.

Personal skills and qualities   This section of your resumé gives you the opportunity to list skills and qualities that are unique to you. List those characteristics that you think will make you qualified for the position you're seeking. For example, if you will be working with a diverse group of clients, you will want to list any foreign language skills you may have. Also, list your computer skills. The importance of being computer-literate, even if it's just possessing word-processing skills, can't be overstated.

Educational background In this section you will list where you attended college, your date of graduation, and your major. Also, list any courses that will be relevant to the position for which you're applying. For example, if you're going for a job as a part-time bookkeeper, you will want to list any accounting courses you took in school.

References Usually job seekers don't list the names of those individuals who will act as their references on their resumés. It's a good idea, though, to tell a prospective employer that such references are available upon request. Be certain to get the permission of those individuals who will be recommending you for the position. Also, be thoughtful about selecting your references. Ask those individuals, such as a former or present employer, who know you and your work well, and who have positive things to say about your performance on the job.

There is plenty of additional published advice on how to create an effective resumé. Here is a list of just a handful of the guides that will give you a step-by-step look at how to write a resumé. The books can be found at your local libraries and bookstores. If the titles aren't currently available, just tell the clerk the book's title and publisher, and she can get it for you, usually in a couple of days.

Beatty, Richard H. *175 High-Impact Resumés.* New York:

John Wiley & Sons, 1996.

Betrus, Michael, and Jay A. Block. *101 Resumés*. New York: McGraw-Hill, 1997.

Ireland, Susan. *The Complete Idiot's Guide to the Perfect Resumé*. New York: MacMillan, 1996.

Don't forget, however: Be sure to get someone whose opinion you respect to review your resumé and cover letter, the more input the better.

YOUR COVER LETTER

Although jaded job seekers swear that employers don't read cover letters, these remain an essential part of the job seeker's portfolio. The most efficient way to distribute a cover letter is to write one, then tailor it a bit to each employer. The cover letter should be one part resumé in paragraph form and one part additional information, such as when you are available to start work, how many hours you can commit to, and perhaps a short sentence or two explaining why finding a part-time job is important.

One note on organization: Keep a copy of every resumé you send or fax. Then, devise a system for organizing your search. You should always be aware of whom you have approached, and to what end. You should know whom you have or have not contacted about the resumé you sent. You should keep a notebook, with a page for each contact, and update it every time you call or fax. Also, you should keep a folder of cover letters, which should be dated, and make notes on each one, so you remember when to follow up and what to say. Typically, you should call one week after you send your resumé. You might use a form like this one to keep track:

Company	Job Description	Sent Resumé (date)	Followed Up (date)	Notes

YOUR CALENDAR

Think about how much time you want to spend searching for a job before you take one. As you proceed, this schedule will be redefined. Keep your goals clear, but be flexible. You might love a job you thought you would hate, and vice versa. When it comes down to it, a plan is imperative, but intuition should have the final say.

EMPLOYMENT AGENCIES

Meeting with a headhunter or employment agent can be useful, especially for part-time job seekers in professional fields. Often, employment counselors can help you answer questions you haven't even thought to ask yourself. They can help determine the best opportunity for your particular situation. If you decide to work with an employment agency, choose it carefully, and pay great attention to how they treat you. Some employment agents are experts, and can be quite nurturing. Others are simply doing their jobs. Some agents will avail themselves for consultation about jobs you found without their help. Some will make you pass typing tests, computer tests, editing tests, then turn you away or never call again. Register with a few to start with and stick with the one that feels the most personal. Older companies usually have solid reputations, but so do some new ones. As with most things, the biggest is not always the best.

TEMPORARY AGENCIES

Temporary agencies are best suited to part-time work, and can be the ideal place to begin a part-time career. The worker determines his or her own hours and accepts each job on an individual basis. Salaries usually range from $8–20 per hour. Office skills and experience are highly regarded in temporary positions, but temp positions can run the gamut from clerical work to sales to handing out flyers on the street corner. Ironically, temping has become one of the most stable sources of income in America. According to the U.S. Department of Labor, the number of temporary agencies has grown at a rate of 20 percent per year for more than twenty years. Manpower, Inc., the largest temporary staffing service in the nation, employs twice as many people as General Motors. According to the National Association of Temporary Staffing Services (NATSS), in a recent year there were more than two million temporary workers in the nation, and that figure is still growing.

Choosing a temporary agency is like choosing any other type of employment agency. Look around, ask friends and family members who have temporary-work experience and which agency they prefer. Check the yellow pages under "Employment contractors—Temporary help," or search the Internet with the key terms *employment, opportunities, temporary, agencies*. When you contact temporary agencies, ask these crucial questions: Does this agency have enough work to keep me as busy as I want to be?

Does it charge me or my future employer? Does it seem interested in helping me find work? Is this agency recommended by its own temporary employees?

CHOOSE WISELY

Choose a temporary agency for what that agency can do for you. Some of the larger agencies can be useful for beginning temps who are learning the ropes and need more assignments in a shorter period of time. But smaller agencies offer more individual attention and more attentive counseling, and though work might start out slow, they are usually more invested in finding you the assignments that fit your individual needs.

BE GOOD TO YOUR AGENCY, AND IT WILL BE GOOD TO YOU

Some temporary agencies offer health care benefits and vacation time to their long-term workers. These more permanent-type temps are sometimes called *staffers*. Fostering a good relationship with your agency is paramount. The amount of work you receive is usually proportional to the amount of praise you receive per assignment from your employer. When a temporary employer praises your work, suggest that she pass the praise along to your agency. Your agency keeps careful track of your progress; after all, your work reflects on your agency's reputation and determines how many companies use their services.

If you prove to be a valuable employee, even on one assignment, an agency will be more willing to assign you additional work and to make concessions concerning your particular schedule. If your sole reason for temping is the extra money, it is a good idea to be as impressive as possible so that an agency will gladly put you on or off the schedule, depending on your need for extra cash, at any time. Inevitably, some conflicts arise between temp workers and their temporary employers. When tension occurs and cannot be rectified, it is best to notify your agency of the problem. This way, if they receive a poor review of your performance, they can take your side of the story into account. According to the NATSS, 38 percent of temps report having been offered full-time positions while working on a temporary assignment. (See chapter 4 for advice on how to turn your part-time job into a full-time career.) This statistic suggests that in many cases, the discomfort that can go along with temping is minimal, and the experience can be very rewarding.

IS TEMPORARY WORK INTERESTING?

Though most temporary work assignments are not usually creative or necessarily interesting, many creative and artistic people temp for a living. Most assignments are office-oriented and can include assisting a CEO (chief executive officer) at a large financial company, or answering phones at a record company. Every once in a while, temp agencies might get more lively requests—for example, one temporary agency in New York City organized a group of workers to take coats at Donald Trump's birthday party. Another group was assigned to hold seats at a Philharmonic concert in the park for employees at an investment firm. Temp agencies can specialize, for example, in legal or medical office work. Often, the environments are more interesting than the work: on Monday, you may be filing bank records, but Tuesday you may be filing art catalogs at a museum. Temporary work is popular among artists, writers, actors, and actresses who go on assignments during the day and pursue their creative initiatives at night. These same people might be the ones who can most easily pull an all-night shift at a moment's notice, and therefore make valuable temporary employees.

RESUMÉ BUILDING

For persons looking to build a more profitable future, temping is a great way to build your resumé and gain experience. You should have some basic typing and computer skills before expecting the better assignments, but the experience you can gain on the job is invaluable. Temping also provides an insider's view of various industries and environments, and can help you make difficult decisions about what sorts of offices you prefer. It can narrow the focus for people with a variety of interests. However, if you're seeking to compensate for a lack of office camaraderie at your full-time job, you should be forewarned that temps often feel left out of office socializing. If you find yourself in this situation, you might want to concentrate on the work rather than on feelings of isolation. Chances are, if you become a valuable part of the office, you will be accepted as a member of the team. However, this might not happen until your assignment is nearing a close.

Two of the largest temporary staffing services in the country are Career Blazers (phone: 888-227-3372) and Manpower Temporary Services (phone: 800-558-6996). For local temporary agencies, consult the yellow pages. There is more information about Internet resources for temporary work in the following section.

THE INTERNET

It is possible to find a job without the aid of the Internet—indeed, people have been doing so for quite a while—but if you have access to a computer that's online, you may want to use it. The Internet is the fastest-growing networking and career resource center in the world. Regardless, the Internet alone will not guarantee you a job. It is a powerful resource to be combined with the others detailed in this book. There are dozens of reasons to use the Internet, but four stand out.

Its Growth Rate   The Internet is growing faster than any library or career center. It is also the only real-time job resource. This means that as soon as information is available, rather than going through the process of publication and distribution, the Internet can publish almost instantly, and to a growing audience. Also, employment resources can post their listings as soon as they are available. Internet job resources are ones you will want to check every few days.

Its Hours   If you are looking for a job while you already have one, chances are you don't have that much free time during the nine-to-five work day. The Internet is available twenty-four hours a day. Of course, you'll still have to squeeze in interviews during your lunch hour.

It Can Save Time   In many ways, using the Internet to find a job can save you time. You don't have to go to the library for job resource books, you don't have to drive to the career center, and you don't have to search hundreds of irrelevant job listings to find the ones you want. On the Internet, you can enter keywords to narrow your search. There are currently more than twelve hundred career-oriented Internet sites. If you aren't careful, and if you don't narrow your search and keep it narrowed, you could waste time. Worse, you could find yourself confused and lost.

Getting access to any one of these Internet sites is often faster than getting to your local library or career center and perusing their career guides. Be careful, though, that you don't become overwhelmed with your Internet searches. Again, keep your searches narrow and focused.

It's Impressive Using the Internet in your job search demonstrates resourcefulness and competence to your potential employer. Telling an employer that you heard about the job on the Internet, rather than in the want ads (even if it is virtually the same thing, in some cases), is impressive, especially these days when being computer-literate is a definite plus.

FOUR TOP JOB RESOURCES ON THE INTERNET

Keep in mind that the number of career-oriented Web sites is overwhelming, and it's growing. Some sites are job listings, some are lists of links to career-oriented sites, some are comprehensive resources resembling online career centers. Most are combinations of all three. The following is a list of some of the best and most popular places to start your search. These sites are particularly helpful for part-time job seekers, although presently there are no comprehensive online resources that concentrate solely on part-time employment. The list is short because each site contains a maze of related links.

What Color Is Your Parachute: The Net Guide
(*www.washingtonpost.com/parachute*)
This is a comprehensive companion guide to Richard Nelson Bolles's popular book of the same name. The

site is sponsored by the Washington Post's Web site, *Washingtonpost.com*. Not only does Bolles's book have a history of respect and popularity, it is a good guide for the part-time job seeker because it offers a holistic approach to the hunt. Bolles also designated what is helpful—and what is not—about the links he recommends.

The Riley Guide *(http://www.dbm.com/jobguide/)*
Highly recommended by many career sites, this page is useful, but would be more so if it included part-time jobs among its specific resource listings. Use this to peruse lists of sites specific to your area of interest—part-time jobs might be waiting there. Also, the Riley Guide has some tips for beginners on using the Internet, and for how to keep your online search effective.

Career Magazine *(http://www.careermag.com/)*
Like a print magazine, this site offers articles about various aspects of the job search, an online columnist ("Ask Alison"), and job openings. Also, at the Career Forum page you can read postings and advice from other Career Magazine readers. This is not the best site for job listings, but the advice is fairly sound, and it is updated regularly.

CareerPath *(http://www.careerpath.com)*
This page offers an exhaustive list of classified ads, searchable by newspaper, job category, and keyword. (Note the Job Category: *Part-time*). This resource is especially helpful for part-time job seekers whose priority is extra income, and for those who are relocating. In any given week in the *New York Times*, for example, there are about fifty part-time jobs advertised. In the

Akron Beacon Journal, there are usually about thirty ads posted. These and other publications' classified ad pages are posted here.

TEMPORARY WORK ONLINE

The best search for temporary employment agencies is in your local yellow pages. If the Internet is somehow more convenient, try Yahoo's Employment section, accessible from Yahoo's main page *(http://www.yahoo.com).* Then search the section with the word *temporary.* This produces several staffing agencies by geographical location. Keep in mind, though, that there is no real shortage of temporary help, which means many agencies lack the impetus to create a Web site.

HELPFUL HINTS

If possible, try to find a job resource that focuses on your geographic area, like Job Smart *(http://jobsmart.org/)* in California, sponsored by the public library system. This has tons of links to job openings in the San Francisco Bay area, Los Angeles, and Sacramento.

Also devise your own list of useful sites by trying a specific search on your favorite search engine. For example, use the terms "waiter/waitress" "cafe" "Manhattan" to find a job waiting tables on weekends; or try "bookstores" "Omaha" "jobs" to find work as a part-time bookstore clerk. Of course, the best approach in these cases is to call or go to your favorite cafes and bookstores to see if they are hiring, but using the Internet may prove successful nonetheless.

Approach companies that intrigue you by going directly to their Web sites. Not only will you educate yourself about the company, and possibly find some interesting interview material, but usually companies advertise their job opportunities on their home pages. Check for linkable buttons called *Jobs, Employment, Join Us,* et cetera.

You might want to create an online resumé for distribution over the Internet. There is not a great deal of proof that online distribution is effective, but considering the growth rate of the Web, posting your resumé may be ultimately worthwhile. Check out the online resumé services of your favorite Internet resource. Your online resumé should follow the rules of a print resumé: it should be clear, concise, professional. An online resumé should fit on fewer than five screens. Although e-mail and the Internet have a fairly informal tone, remember to use Mr. and Ms. in your online correspondence, as you would in paper correspondence.

MISCELLANEOUS SITES

Hoover's Online *(http://www.careermosaic.com/)*
This is the ultimate resource for specific company information. Find out if the company you want to work for has a Web site, whether or not it is hiring, and for what jobs. Since 90 percent of all available jobs are never officially advertised, a company's home page is often a great back door.

CoolWorks *(http://www.coolworks.com/)*
This site specializes in off-the-beaten-path work, which is not the practical part-time option for most. Some of the main focuses are Resort Jobs, Cruise Jobs, Ski Jobs, and Ranch Jobs. Many require travel or summers free.

EPage *(http://www.ep.com/)*
You might stumble across something interesting in this

page's part-time classified listings, though most of it is work from home or pyramid sales.

University of Waterloo's Career Development Manual *(http://www.adm.uwaterloo.ca/infocecs/CRC/manual-home.html)*
Check out the Self-Assessment page at this site if you are having trouble determining your part-time goals, desires, and abilities.

OTHER ONLINE RESOURCES

Job Bank USA *(http://www.jobbankusa.com/)*
Career Mosaic *(http://www.careermosaic.com/)*
Monster Board *(http://www.monster.com)*
Online Career Center *(http://www.occ.com/)*
Catapult *(http://www.jobweb.org/catapult/catapult.htm)*

FREELANCING

Starting a successful freelancing business is not easy, but there are a couple of ways to encourage interest in your work.

CREATE A PORTFOLIO

No matter the medium of your work—whether it is illustrations, writing, design, or photographs—you should have a neat, professional portfolio in which to display your work. Divide the portfolio into categories by date, style, or assignment. If you are a confident photographer, compile your best photographs and circulate an abridged version of your portfolio to friends and family. Offer to work half-price until the work gets rolling. Weddings, bar mitzvahs, and graduations are accessible opportunities to work and build your portfolio. You can create a winning portfolio no matter what your field, providing you have a little experience. Writers should include work of every relevant genre; actors should include head shots and detailed descriptions of past work; graphic designers should include as many distinct examples of their work as possible.

DISCIPLINE YOURSELF

It may seem obvious, but the most important aspect of a successful freelancing business is *working*. If you're starting out with little experience, solicit and accept whatever work you can. The more you have in your portfolio, the longer your resumé, the more attractive you will be as a freelancer. Designate time during the day or week to your projects and developing clients, and stick to your time frame. If you don't have any contracted assignments, assign some to yourself. Work on these self-contracted assignments, then distribute them to relevant parties. Very few people just happen upon a successful freelancing business. Most freelancers work hard and long before they generate enough work to be comfortable, not to mention self-supporting.

Take a look at Freelance Online (*http://www.freelanceonline. com*), an Internet resource for freelancers in publishing. (Keep in mind, though, that there are as many types of freelancing jobs as there are regular jobs, and they range as much in salary.) Also check out the *Job Opportunities* page at Telecommuting Jobs (*http://www.tjobs.com/*).

VOLUNTEERING

If you are in need of extra income, volunteering is clearly not the way to go, though many volunteer positions can evolve into full- or part-time jobs. More people than you would think carry on full volunteering lives, above and beyond their full-time careers. Volunteering is ideal for people whose nine-to-five jobs are not gratifying, personally or socially. Volunteering is a great way to contribute to the community and meet new people. Coaching a local children's soccer team, for example, can be very fulfilling, but is usually unpaid. Animal lovers can volunteer as little as three hours per week at their local ASPCA. Volunteers at FROST'D in New York City distribute condoms and free HIV tests to prostitutes.

Volunteering can be a valuable way to evaluate your part-time trajectory and to determine how many hours a week to devote to a part-time job, if and when you are ready for the commitment. Most volunteers devote two to six shifts per month to their organizations.

Many volunteer organizations are discriminating employers and require rigorous training programs before allowing a volunteer to work. Usually, training programs consist of several classes spaced over a few weeks. Afterward, a volunteer has usually acquired valuable resumé material and a new skill set, not to mention the overall satisfaction of volunteering. One female volunteer we spoke with works 45–55 hours a week as a computer-gaming specialist in an all-male office, then spends one or two nights a week volunteering at the ASPCA, among more than a dozen coworkers, most of them women. This is just one example of what a dramatically different experience volunteering can be.

VOLUNTEER RESOURCES ONLINE

The best way to find a job volunteering is to simply choose an organization that interests you and call. Volunteer opportunities are usually posted at local public libraries.

Also, many cities run their own volunteer coalitions, like New York City's Mayoral Volunteer Task Force. Many local colleges hold free one-session classes about volunteer opportunities in the area. Chances are, someone you know has had a great volunteer job, or knows of one that might be right for you.

For general information and a survey of what is available, in terms of volunteering opportunities, check out these Web sites:

Impact Online *(http://www.impactonline.org)*
This site has a list of volunteering opportunities, but it is by no means an exhaustive one. Search by geographical area. Also, note the Virtual Volunteering section— an expanding database of volunteer projects you can work on from home or office, via the Internet.

P&G Volunteer Resource Bank
(http://www.pg.com/community/volunteer_links/)
The most comprehensive list of volunteer and nonprofit links on the Web.

CAREER BOOKS

As most people this far along in the job hunt usually realize, there are not a lot of current books on how to develop or organize your part-time career. The following books are relevant to the part-time job seeker, should you hit any insurmountable obstacles along the way:

Boldt, Laurence. *Zen and the Art of Making a Living: A Practical Guide to Creative Career Design.* New York: Penguin USA, 1993.
Though it seems a bit old, this book is meaty, uplifting, and imaginative.

Cook, Mary F. *Consulting on the Side: How to Start a Part-*

Time Consulting Business While Still Working at Your Full-Time Business. New York: John Wiley & Sons, 1996.

The Directory of Executive Temporary Placement Firms. Fitzwilliam, N.H.: Kennedy Publications, 1995.

A directory of temporary firms that specialize in executive placement. Lists each company's geographic area and industries served.

Eikleberry, Carol. *The Career Guide for Creative and Unconventional People.* Berkeley, CA.: Ten Speed Press, 1995.

This is a great source for anyone looking to use their creative talents in their part-time work. Includes creative career choices, creative self-employment, and even an appendix of creative job descriptions.

Faux, Marian. *Successful Freelancing: The Complete Guide to Establishing and Running Any Kind of Freelance Business.* New York: St. Martin's Press, 1996.

A step-by-step guide to freelancing, including discussion of legal and official rules and regulations.

Gerberg, Bob. *An Easier Way to Change Jobs.* Princeton: Princeton Masters Press, 1993.

Contains some useful information for people who want to segue into a full-time job.

Hadlely, Joyce. *Part-Time Careers: For Anyone Who Wants More Than Just a Job—but Less Than a Forty-Hour Week!* Franklin Lakes, N.J.: Career Press, 1993.

This substantive book contains information geared toward part-time job seekers without full-time careers, and includes valuable information about employment agencies and freelance work.

The Job Seeker's Guide to Online Resources. Fitzwilliam, N.H.: Kennedy Publications, 1995.

This is a no-nonsense list of online career resources on the World Wide Web.

Lacquer, Maria and Donna Dickinson. *Breaking Out of Nine-to-Five: How to Redesign Your Job to Fit You.* Princeton: Peterson's, 1994.

This book explores the various alternatives to full-time career life, like telecommuting, permanent part-time work, compressing your work week, temping, and job sharing. The content is practical and very specific.

Radin, Bill. *Breakaway Careers: The Self-Employment Resource for Freelancers, Consultants, and Corporate Refugees.* Franklin Lakes, N.J.: Career Press, 1994.

Radin writes from experience about developing an untraditional career. The book is easy to follow and very practical.

Rogers, Richard. *Temping: The Insider's Guide.* New York: Arco Books, Macmillan USA, 1996.

Again, if these books are not available at your bookstore or library, ask your bookstore manager or librarian about how they can obtain the book for you.

We've told you how you can go about seeking and obtaining your ideal part-time job. But none of our advice is going to matter if you don't have an essential quality that all job seekers must possess: a positive mental attitude. Believe in yourself, and you will get the job of your dreams.

◆ ◆ ◆

Fingers in Lots of Pies:
Stephen's Story

The first time Stephen, thirty-four, found himself in need of some extra cash, he was twenty-four years old. He was then working full-time as a waiter in his college town of Atlanta, Georgia. Ever ambitious, he returned to his college career center and combed the part-time job listings. Many of the listings were right up his alley.

"They had listings for nannies and baby-sitters, dog walkers, editors and writers, administrative support, anything you could think of," Stephen said.

Since it is usually free to register a local job with a university's career center, Stephen had access to a wide range of hours, salaries, and types of work. In his case, he needed to pick up a simple, flexible, moderately paid part-time job for weekends and off-hours. He did better than find a suitable part-time position, however—he found two!

"At the career center there was this great posting by a local yogurt shop advertising an opening. They only needed me three shifts a week, for five hours a shift. It was perfect because I could prove I had experience working in a restaurant, but the work wasn't as difficult as the restaurant job. I could work a five-hour shift at the yogurt place and still have plenty of energy to pull a late night—and get lots of tips—at my waiting job."

Three months after he began working at the yogurt shop, Stephen landed his second part-time job. A friend mentioned he needed some administrative help at his medical office one day a week. "I remember he was so frustrated trying to fill this position. He said to me, 'Do you know how hard it is to find someone who is free just one day a week?' I said, 'I'm free!'"

So, having earned the esteem of the superiors at both his jobs, he could finagle one day every week to help at his friend's office. Though Stephen had a minimum of experience with anything outside food service, he could handle general administrative duties such as filing, answering the phone, and confirming appointments, as well as some light bookkeeping.

"I think in one day of that job I made more money than in a week at the restaurant—two weeks at the yogurt place! No, that's an exaggeration. But it was good money. I was working all the time, and I liked it. I had my fingers in a lot of pies."

He also gained valuable work experience. Having juggled three jobs—especially with strong references and recommendations—makes a valuable impression on future employers. Stephen could communicate, simply by summarizing a week of his life, that he was responsible, punctual, a hard worker, and had the drive to succeed.

Maybe Stephen could have handled three jobs for more than one year if he had been given the chance. Fortunately for him, he wasn't.

"I was the youngest person to be offered a position as a manager at my restaurant," he said. "It wasn't what I saw myself doing in five years, but it was a lot more money, and it meant I could make some progress in my career."

And progress he made. With a couple of years' experience managing a restaurant—managing anything, for that matter—Stephen gained the skills and resumé material, not to mention the connections, to carve a niche for himself in the field of his choice. He gave up the office job. Though he hadn't expected to, he was enjoying restaurant management.

"The restaurant I'd been working in was a family-style chain restaurant," he said. "I liked the work, but I wasn't crazy about the place itself. I was always having to deal with other managers and new staff, and the atmosphere was stale."

So began Stephen's second stint into the arena of multi-job juggling. He took a part-time assistant-manager position at a nearby dessert-style coffeehouse, which he found by inquiring about openings at his favorite restaurants.

"The atmosphere at the new place was much more amenable to my tastes," he said. "I worked evenings and cut back a little on my daytime schedule, so I really wasn't making much more money on the whole. But I was gaining more experience in the restaurant management field, which was important because it is a competitive one."

Stephen reached a point where he had been juggling both management positions for one year. He was quite happy with his work at the dessert place—sales were up, the staff was happier than ever, and he felt like he had learned a great deal in his short time working there. Unfortunately, there was little chance at turning his part-time job into a full-time one, since the restaurant was owned and managed by the same family, and the best positions were reserved for relatives. He was also growing more frustrated with his full-time job, and he was receiving increasing pressure to take on more responsibility there.

"At this point, I was twenty-nine years old," Stephen said, "and I was moving vaguely in the direction I wanted to move. But I felt that if I didn't make a change, I was going to get stuck."

Although Stephen had more experience and resources, the job hunt this time around was more difficult since his expectations were higher. "I was past the point where I could just pick up any old job and work my butt off. I needed to add to my resumé, to increase my marketability. To top it off, I was thinking it might be time for a change of scenery."

This change of scenery took six months to come to fruition. Still working hard at both jobs, Stephen put together his first resumé in years. "I had to decide precisely what I wanted. I wrote two resumés—one to break into a field I hadn't broken into yet, which was catering and restaurant consulting. The second one was one for other restaurant positions."

Stephen decided he wanted to move back to his hometown of Manhattan. "New York City is full of restaurants, so in that respect it was a good move for me. On the other hand, the city is full of restaurateurs, so I had heavy competition," he said.

For three months, Stephen diligently combed the *New York Times* and the *Daily News* classifieds for restaurant openings. He was either overqualified or underqualified for all of them. Except one.

"I got called to go on this great interview for a position managing a small neighborhood cafe that served lunch, dinner, and dessert," he said. "It was perfect in ever way, except that they didn't hire me." After that disappointment, as well as the $300 plane ticket to travel to the interview, he called it quits with the classifieds. "I still glanced through them on Sundays, but I began to concentrate more on contacts. I'm from New York, so I had some people I could call."

The response he received was surprising. "I thought I didn't know anyone involved in the restaurant business. But it turned out I didn't need to—I knew people who knew people in the business." The next time Stephen flew to New York, it was to move there. Through his ex-roommate's sister's friend, he was hired as a manager at a small restaurant in Greenwich Village. But there was a catch—the job was only a part-time one, with room to move into full-time, eventually.

"It was perfect," Stephen said, "because it got me to the place I wanted to be, and left me room to work on my consulting resumé."

After an adjustment period of six months, Stephen

enrolled in a culinary class. Then another, and another. Eventually, he took over all the ordering of pastries and desserts in the restaurant, and he made a name for himself with the restaurant's owner by developing an entirely new and creative menu. Soon, Stephen landed his first consulting job with a new catering company. Again, he found himself working two jobs. "Sometimes I don't remember a time when I had fewer than two jobs at once," he said. "I'm all over the place, and I like it!"

✦ ✦ ✦

Focus and Persistence— Keys to Making Your Dream Career a Reality: Allison's Story

Allison, thirty, is presently working on her third full-length feature film script. But since she graduated from college at age twenty-two, she has held her fair share of part- and full-time jobs in a variety of fields and for a gamut of salaries.

"When I got out of college, I had no idea what I wanted to do," Allison said. "So I got my diploma and continued working at the same place where I'd worked throughout school—a local retail clothing store."

Allison had to double her hours, working overtime most nights, to cover rent in her hometown of Ann Arbor, Michigan. She was bored and frustrated. A closet screenwriter, Allison found herself with no time, or energy, left to write. "I was feeling stifled in Ann Arbor, and at my old job. I was overripe for a big change."

She saved just enough money to move to Los Angeles, the filmmaking capital of the world. She slept on a friend's floor for two weeks, with barely enough time to find a job and a place to live. She had intended to find a position working for a studio or screenwriter, but there didn't seem to be any openings. A short step away from running out of money completely, Allison took a position with a temporary agency, relying on the typing and people skills she had learned in college and at the clothing store.

"I discovered that with the temp assignments during the day, I had plenty of time to work on my screenplay at night. I could even write during work sometimes, if all I was doing was answering phones."

After several months of temping and developing a relationship with her temp agency, Allison was assigned a one-week stint working as a secretary at a talent agency. "I was surrounded by all this talent, all those budding screenwriters, but all I was doing was taking dictation, faxing, and answering phones," she said.

That didn't last long. The day before her job was going to end, the director of the agency offered her a full-time position as a secretary. "I was thrilled, but frustrated," she said. "I couldn't help feeling like I had gotten the wrong foot in the right door."

To top it off, Allison's new job barely paid enough to cover the rent of her small studio apartment. She had to find another source of income. "My options were few," she said. "I thought about waitressing, but that is so tiring. I wouldn't have enough energy to have a full-time job, wait tables, and write as well. And there was nothing available in my field, unless I wanted to take an unpaid internship. This was L.A.—there were plenty of people willing to work for free just to get started."

One day, Allison saw a help wanted sign in the window of a neighborhood health club. "It was a gym I'd wanted to join but couldn't afford," she said. "When I saw the sign I knew I wanted the job. A job there meant extra money plus a free membership."

Allison got the position and right away began working four shifts, three on week nights and one on the weekend. She stayed a half hour after each shift to get some exercise. "I was busier than ever, but I felt happier," she said. "I was getting something in return. I could justify my low salary at the talent agency because it was a way to break into the business, and I was making extra money on the side, and getting to use a great gym for free. I found that although I had very little free time, I was more motivated to write."

This continued for two years. Eventually, Allison was promoted, but not by the talent agency. "The gym made me an aerobics instructor. When I started there I didn't know anything about aerobics, but I had picked up almost every routine, plus I had a few of my own. I didn't have the credentials, but my manager was confident in my abilities."

Her aerobics class ran three days a week, at six o'clock in the morning. "It was an awful hour of the day. But it was a lot of money, and it meant I had plenty of time after work to write. Finally, my real work was coming along."

When it was complete, her screenplay was 145 pages long, and she had been working on it for almost five years. Having been a secretary at the talent agency for more than three years at this point, Allison made her move. "One day I got up the courage to ask my boss for the favor of looking at my work. The next day I handed her this fat manuscript. She was surprised, to say the least."

Allison admits she could have been more assertive throughout her time at the agency. She could have accepted the full-time position with the agreement that her boss would, from time to time, take a look at her work. Instead, she dumped a completed manuscript in her boss's lap with little prior warning. "It was weeks before she got around to reading the manuscript," Allison said, "and more weeks before she gave me any feedback. That was really hard. She wanted to take me seriously as a writer, but I had never asserted my interest before. Once she realized I was serious, she gave me some real feedback."

She gave Allison more than that. Because of her promising script, the agency agreed to pay for 75 percent of Allison's tuition for a screenwriting class at a nearby college. With some formal training under her belt, Allison was able to work with her boss to perfect the script. After a great deal of grueling editing, her own agency agreed to represent her. She was on her way.

But Allison was on her way not only because of her talent and the attention given to her and her work at the college and by her manager. Allison was on her way because she remained, ever since her days in Ann Arbor, Michigan, focused on her career as a screenwriter. She worked to make her dream of becoming a screenwriter a reality. "I knew I would never feel happy or fulfilled, personally and professionally, if I couldn't be a screenwriter. I was confident in my abilities to succeed in the field. But I had to be persistent and focused on achieving my goal. Like they say, success is ninety percent perspiration and ten percent inspiration. That has certainly been the case with me."

✦ ✦ ✦

2

THE BALANCING ACT
How to Hold Down
Two Jobs *and* Your Stress

Now that you've obtained the second job that best meets your goals and expectations, you have no doubt come to appreciate its personal and financial rewards. But there is one downside to holding down a second job—balancing your new responsibilities with your old ones. And, as those of us who have had second jobs know, this is no easy task. Once you've acquired the skills to find the balance between your personal and professional lives, you'll find having a second job is just as fulfilling as you had hoped. This chapter will teach you those skills, and much more, so that having a second job will become a positive addition to your life, not a negative one.

For those of us who have more than one job, "I'm so stressed" is probably the most highly used phrase both in and out of the workplace. But what do we mean when we say we're stressed? Often, when we say we are stressed we are saying we have a lot on our minds because we are juggling too many projects simultaneously. Stress is very real and can have adverse effects on our physical and psychological well-being, often impeding productivity and creativity, as well as on our personal relationships. Being in a constant state of stress results in feeling overwhelmed, anxious, and out of control. These feelings can affect us both emotionally and physically.

People who work more than one job can be in a state of perpetual stress, particularly if they push both their minds and bodies to harmful limits without outlets for such strain. Although many people say they find their outlets in their second, or even primary, jobs, participating in their life's passion, these very people are likely candidates for burnout—a point where they feel they have completely run out of steam. Burnout means they are often in a constant state of fatigue, both physically and mentally, and are no longer able to give energy to their careers or their personal lives.

Stress can begin when we feel that there are too many things going on at once. We have too many responsibilities, no personal time, no time to do the things we once found fun—feelings we all have from time to time. However, if these feelings of being overwhelmed persist over long periods of time, they begin to manifest themselves in our physical well-being by affecting our sleeping and eating patterns and our social interaction with friends, family, and colleagues.

But this doesn't have to be the case. By following a few simple rules outlined in this chapter, and keeping focused, you'll be able to keep that second job and lead a life that you will find rewarding and satisfying.

"TWO JOBS. WHAT, ME WORRY?"

As we've already discussed, people take on second jobs for many different reasons. There are those who work a full-time job simply to pay the bills and take a second job that is more aligned with their future goals and dreams. Actors, models, writers, comedians—people who want to succeed in the world of entertainment or the arts—are likely candidates for working multiple jobs, often waiting tables, or taking on temp jobs, or freelancing in other areas, depending on their qualifications. There are also people who take on the responsibility of two jobs due to financial reasons; they need or would like extra money. Maybe the income from the second job is going toward a decadent vacation, or for savings for a child's education. Others take on another line of work because it feeds their interests, and it may be fun.

Those of us who have a second job that takes us into realms that we always dreamed of have it easier in some ways. For instance, an artist who works as a clerk everyday, but performs as a dancer in a theater group at night is less prone to be stressed than the person who has the same clerical job and also waits tables in a restaurant before his day is done. In the second example, there is no creative outlet. That person may not have a passion for either of the two jobs, just a need for the money earned from working at both.

There are different levels of stress for every individual. Each person must take the time to look at herself and appraise where they are in terms of all the other elements in their lives that are shifting as a result of a second job. But whatever the case may be, all people who work two or more jobs simultaneously need to step back every so often to evaluate their lives and see if they are not overstepping the boundaries necessary for living healthy, happy lives. Stress can be managed, but only if it does not go unnoticed. In the following pages we will explore the boundaries we need to set in order to maintain healthy personal and professional lives. In order to define our boundaries, we first need to get to know ourselves a little better.

WHAT CAUSES STRESS

There are many factors that contribute to stress—and it's not the second job alone. What ultimately causes stress is the impact having the second job has on our time, relationships, and health. Some of the most important elements are time, organization, focus, and priorities. Each element, at one point or other, affects the others. For example, the use of our time becomes completely rearranged with a shift in lifestyle, changing the way we normally focus and prioritize, and so on.

In order to get these elements under control, we need to look at each part of the equation separately and see what we need to consider when confronted with the challenges of the stress of suddenly having two jobs.

THERE'S NEVER ENOUGH TIME

"Aaargh! I had no idea having a second job would take so much time away from my family. I don't even have time for myself!" "I haven't seen a movie in months, or had a date with my girlfriend." If you feel these might be causes of concern once you've taken on a second job, you're not alone. All of us with second jobs have said almost the same things. As the new job becomes an integral part of your life, you need to consider the amount of time that is being spent at the job, thinking and planning for that job, and, ultimately, what activities are lost because of this job. Even if it's time spent in front of the TV, something is being neglected in order to put energy into your new responsibility. Take a step back and evaluate your present life circumstances and schedule. If the new job takes precedence over important physical, mental, and social elements in your life, such as sleep or time spent with your spouse and family, the new situation obviously will be neither a happy nor healthy one and will lead to stress. To allow the second job to overwhelm your schedule could prove to be destructive to your physical and psychological health, as well as affect important relationships in your life. If this becomes the case, you may want to reconsider the part-time job you took on. You should perhaps look for a position that is less taxing, or one that requires you to work fewer hours. Or, if your boss is asking you to work more hours than you'd expected, speak to her in a professional manner about how to schedule you for fewer hours during the week.

ORGANIZATION IS KEY

Tom volunteered at a local homeless shelter and held down a part-time job as a temp at a law firm. While he was at the law firm one evening, Tom realized he had forgotten he'd promised the director of the volunteer group that he would give a hand at the soup kitchen that night. He didn't realize his mistake until after the dinner hour at the soup kitchen, too late to call the soup kitchen's director and apologize. He felt awful.

Keeping your schedule in check and using your time efficiently requires organization, a skill Tom hadn't yet acquired when he took on the responsibilities at the soup kitchen. Maintain personal and official deadlines, or you'll face serious cramming and conflicts, particularly with two jobs. Keep personal appointments such as doctor's visits, veterinary visits, anniversaries, and birthdays of friends and family neatly jotted down in a personal organizer or digital datebook. A calendar would also be helpful in this regard. When your schedule leaves you little room, you'll be glad you took the time to note these activities and avoided disappointing others by forgetting about your personal obligations.

Studies show that the more organized a person is, the more likely that person will be to meet with success. If you're feeling as if your life is in a state of disarray with a second job, look at how you spend each day. A good place to start is by choosing any three days during a typical week. Keep track of the way you spend your time during these three days. Record your activities for each day on a piece of paper. Be certain to write the time you began and ended each activity.

Now that you've done that, look it over closely. Where did you tend to waste time? Where and how could you spend your time more efficiently? Write down answers to these questions to get a good and honest account of your day.

Each day you should create a "to-do list." It could look something like this:

Day _____   Date _____

Task to be completed	When	Done	Notes

_____

_____

_____

Be certain to note when each item needs to be completed. Also, keep this list with you at all times and use it every day. When you see your deadlines and errands in writing, you'll feel less overwhelmed. Check things off once you've completed the errand or project. This activity will help you feel as if you have accomplished a goal, a sort of reward. Once you've started checking off items on your list, you'll see that the other items to be completed that day are becoming more manageable.

When creating your list, be realistic. Don't state that you're going to complete a major project in a single day. Break it into separate assignments to avoid feelings of being overwhelmed and inadequate.

FIND YOUR FOCUS

Sally often found herself daydreaming while at her secretarial job. For example, she would think about the inventory lists for her evening job at the boutique, instead of the filing that needed to be done.

Always focus on what's at hand. Since you'll find that you have at least two or more separate sets of responsibilities—one for each job—in addition to your personal commitments, you'll need to maintain your focus on whatever you are engaged in at each particular moment. Don't go through your day job preoccupied with your evening or weekend responsibilities, or vice versa. This will kill your efficiency.

Always try to keep your two jobs separate. The last

thing you need to do is to upset your employer by showing him or her that your attention is elsewhere, especially at another job. For example, if you're a freelance writer with an office day job, try not to bring in your manuscript and work on it during the day. It's unavoidable, especially when you have pending deadlines, but as much as possible, remember to keep the jobs separate.

You may hear people say, "he's so focused." Have you ever thought about exactly what that meant? Why is being focused so applauded and deemed such a compliment? Well, focus is about being completely engaged with whatever project you've taken on. Usually, a focused person does not miss little details, doesn't make mistakes, and uses his or her time efficiently. When you lose focus, it takes time to get back into what you're doing.

Having two jobs takes getting used to, and learning to maintain your focus at each job takes practice. Make a mental note of your tendency to lose focus and when you find yourself drifting and losing attention. Make an effort to snap back into focus what you're supposed to be doing at a particular moment. Think of yourself as a camera taking in an entire landscape. Instead of trying to capture the entire scenery into one blurry picture where the setting is barely visible, focus on the details you want to capture separately. Take two separate pictures where you can see the details of the landscape, instead of one sloppy one. Being focused is a learned discipline, one that's handy when you have many priorities to juggle.

PRIORITIZE YOUR OBLIGATIONS

It's near the end of the workday, and Claire is looking forward to her company's party that would take place that night at a fancy restaurant in town. She decides to check in with her boyfriend to confirm their date for the party. But Mike, her boyfriend, tells her something she doesn't want to hear.

"Claire, honey, I know I told you I'd come to your company party, but I have to stay here and finish up this project," he says.

"But, Mike, you postponed our date last week as well. Every time we make plans, something comes up at work, or you find something else that takes priority over me."

"I know, I'm sorry," says Mike. "I'll make it up to you, I promise."

Claire sighs. "But you always say that and you never do."

No matter how much you learn to focus, sometimes you will not be able to do everything you want to do. Mike has taken on too many responsibilities at work, and has let his girlfriend down in the process. Do not let the things that are important in your life take a back seat to all the work you've laid out for yourself. This requires you to prioritize your commitments and responsibilities.

Having two jobs and a personal life is harder than it sounds. No matter how much you try, your priorities will occasionally overlap, forcing you to make tough decisions you'd rather avoid. If and when that does happen, you need to sit down and look at what is most important, and decide what can wait. For example, if you have an anniversary coming up, and you're scheduled to work that same evening, sit down, if possible, with your supervisor or boss at work, and tell her about the important event in your life that's coming up. Plan ahead, though. Don't wait until the last minute to spring such news on your boss.

Do not take your personal time and the people in your life for granted. You can only expect others to be understanding for so long, so do not assume that your personal life is where you should be whittling time away. You'll soon be left empty-handed.

By getting organized and setting priorities you can keep that second job and lead a well-rounded life. It's okay to deviate from your calendar every so often, but do so rarely and only as a reward for your hard work. Straying from your calendar too often may become a habit and lead to stress.

DETECTING—AND ALLEVIATING—STRESS

There are times, however, when even the best organized person feels overwhelmed by stress. It's essential, then, that you recognize and alleviate its symptoms, which include headaches, fatigue, irritability, forgetfulness, weight fluctuation, acne or rashes, insomnia or fitful sleep, and anxiety.

Stress, like any condition, has telltale signs. Often, these signs are physical, but at other times they are manifested in behavior. It's important to know that for each person the symptoms may differ, and not every individual suffering from stress will necessarily have all of the above symptoms. In fact, you may not have any of these symptoms. Instead, you may have ones that are less common.

It's easiest to detect when you are overly burdened with work-related tensions and when you know yourself and your body well enough to notice changes that are symptomatic of a serious case of stress. It's always a good idea to go for regular check-ups with a physician who is familiar with your medical history and lifestyle. The best and surest advice in detecting and alleviating symptoms of stress is: know yourself and take care of yourself!

HEADACHES

"I have such a headache!" is probably the most loudly heard complaint of stressed people. Headaches and migraines are the body's way of saying that it has reached its threshold for mental and physical strain. Migraines are much more severe than headaches. The difference between a migraine and a headache is that migraines attack suddenly and are usually confined to one side of the head and are usually associated with nausea. Headaches are generally milder and easier to alleviate.

If you notice that you have recurring headaches, or ones common painkillers can't relieve, you should reassess the lifestyle you've carved out for yourself since taking on a second job.

Evaluate your life and see if you are getting enough rest, and if your diet is sufficient and healthy. You may simply be neglecting yourself physically. Most important, take an honest look at your new schedule and ask yourself if you might have accepted too many responsibilities with another job, or if perhaps you are not prioritizing your responsibilities in an effective way. The headaches may be telling you something you don't want to think about.

FATIGUE

Michelle is constantly feeling tired. Recently, she took herself to a movie and fell asleep in the middle of it. When she was on the bus ride home from her part-time job, she also fell asleep. Like many people who have part-time jobs, Michelle is feeling fatigued.

If you find that you are reaching a state where you are physically incapable of carrying on with your daily routine, or if after getting out of bed you never feel fully rested, you are probably suffering from fatigue. Assess sleeping habits and patterns. Later in the chapter, we will discuss insomnia and stress-related sleep disorders. If you think you may be suffering from Chronic Fatigue Syndrome, you should look at your sleep patterns as well as the other health-related symptoms which may be further aggravating your condition, such as diet. You should also make an appointment with your doctor, as Chronic Fatigue Syndrome is a serious matter.

If your sleeping or eating habits have not changed significantly, you may simply be exhausted by all the emotional and mental baggage that comes with your second job. Fatigue may just be your body's way of saying to your mind, "Look, I just can't do as much as you expect from me. You need to slow down so I can keep up with you."

Contrary to what your intuition may tell you, one way to combat fatigue and general lethargy is to increase the amount of exercise in your weekly routine. It's been proven that the more you exercise and the better shape you are in physically, the more energy you have throughout the day, and the less rest your body actually needs. You become more alert and work more efficiently as you reach a higher level of physical wellness.

IRRITABILITY

Ever since he took on the added responsibilities of another job, Tom found himself losing patience with his young children. If they broke something or made a mess, as children often do, he had difficulty getting a grip on his anger and often found himself quick to yell, instead of dealing with the situation calmly and rationally.

No one wants to think of himself as an irritable person.

Situations come up, however, that test our levels of tolerance. When we get angry, we generally like to think we have valid reasons to feel that way. This is generally true, unless we have reached an unhealthy level of stress in our daily routine so that simple problems are amplified. Small grievances then become cause for eruptions and our behavior continues to shift as we become moody, short-tempered, and emotionally volatile.

When we are irritable we react to most given situations with anger, hostility, or simply impatience. If this kind of behavior is not common for you, reassess your schedule. It is often a mismanaged schedule that lends itself to irritable behavior.

If you feel that you have reached that limit where irritability is present in your interaction with colleagues and people close to you, you should certainly take notice. Take an honest look at your lifestyle to see if the irritability came on soon after you took on your second job. Ask the people closest to you whether they have noticed a shift in your behavior. After learning what is contributing to your emotional distress, make the necessary changes in your life to alleviate such emotional stress.

To detect how you might rid yourself of your irritability, look at your schedule and ask yourself these and other questions: Are you getting enough sleep? Have you taken on too many responsibilities? Are you eating well enough? Getting answers to these and other questions, and working to find a balance in your schedule so that it leaves you with time to relax, will help diminish your level of irritability. Keep your answers in a journal. You may also want to ask friends if they've noticed a change in your behavior since you've assumed a part-time job. Their answers may prove enlightening and helpful.

FORGETFULNESS

"I can't remember if I sent around the memo to my bosses," says Sheila quite nervously, leafing through her pile of papers. "I think I did, I remember making a note to do it, but I just can't remember!"

Forgetfulness, oftentimes, is the mind's way of saying, "I'm full and I can't ingest any more." Unless you have reason to think that you may have a serious problem, or a chronic illness that may be affecting your memory, stress may be causing your memory-loss problems. You may simply have "too much on your plate"—too much to remember, too much to worry about, too much activity without enough time to recharge mentally. To avoid being forgetful, keep close track of your itinerary for the day. Cross off items from your list as you complete them.

WEIGHT FLUCTUATIONS

It's easy to develop bad eating habits because, with the loss of extra time, it's difficult to prepare healthy yet tasty, nutritious, and low-fat meals. More than any other time in our lives, we need proper nutrition, now that we are physically and mentally challenging ourselves. Relying on fatty, low-nutrition fast-food is the worst remedy to a very common problem. We often rationalize that there isn't enough time to cook healthy meals, but our diet is not the place to scrimp, in terms of time and effort. Developing bad eating habits because of our work schedule early on may lead to permanent problems.

Weight problems are probably most common for people who feel like there aren't enough hours in a day. These same people often find themselves dining in the office or studio, or wherever their place of work is. This often means ordering in high-fat, high-sodium foods which lack the vitamins and nutrients overworked minds and bodies require to stay on top of our priorities. Although this may seem like the most practical and convenient solution, it's not worth the toll it takes in the long run. Ordering in Chinese food with colleagues once in a while is okay, but we should be wary of developing a habit out of this.

If this has become a habit, take a critical look at your eating pattern. Ask yourself the following questions:

Do you find that it's been a really long time since you sat down for a home-cooked meal?

Do you rarely go out to nice restaurants with friends or family like you used to, grabbing dinner on the run instead?

Is eating no longer something you enjoy, but something that is simply time-consuming and not something that you feel the need to concern yourself with?

Or, on the other extreme:

Do you find yourself seeking solace in food, especially rich, fatty foods, in an attempt to battle the void in your life that your stressful work schedule has created?

Do you simply find eating distasteful now? Do you have no time to worry yourself about it and often "forget" to eat?

If you answered yes to one or more of these questions, or if you simply feel that you aren't eating as healthily as you used to, it's time to evaluate your diet and your relationship with food. Not only do you owe it to yourself to take care of yourself with proper nutrition, but correct eating habits are essential for high efficiency, no matter what your line of work is. In considering the additional stress of your second job, the last thing you will want to do is add more with poor nutrition.

ACNE OR RASHES

Sometimes our skin gives us signs that we are not paying close attention to our bodies and our minds. Particularly when we are in situations of prolonged stress and aggravation, our skin tends to react before we become aware of the problem. Some people develop adult acne under stress, while others develop rashes—usually hives or other skin irritations which can cause itchy discomfort.

While there are over-the-counter cortisone creams and ointments that can give temporary relief to rashes, it's important not to forget that our skin is telling us something. Much like a fever alerts us to an infection, rashes and acne often tell us that we are not taking proper care of ourselves—whether it be a lack of exercise or proper nutrition in our routine.

INSOMNIA OR FITFUL SLEEP

Fitful sleep is often the first sign that we are under too much pressure at work. It's common to have difficulty falling asleep because we can't stop worrying about the following day, an important presentation, or how we're going to fit in all the things we need to do in a single day. We might find ourselves waking up in a panic if we have some unfinished business in the office that needs tending to, or just have bad dreams in which we don't finish what we need to get done. Nightmare situations like this are the brain's normal way of releasing anxiety and are not much source for worrying. But if you're becoming sleep-deprived because you have too many things to worry about, too many tasks you've taken on with your new job and your personal responsibilities, it's time to wake up and smell the coffee. It's especially important to take note if you are beginning to suffer from insomnia.

Sleep deprivation is not only stressful for the body but can make you lose focus and make errors on the job. It's also important to pay particular attention if you are often on the road, driving a vehicle. The statistics for car accidents involving drowsy drivers are higher than you might expect. On the other hand, if you suffer from insomnia, taking over-the-counter medications, like sleeping pills, is not necessarily the right solution. The best thing to do, if you think you may have a sleep problem, is to go to your physician and tell him your problem, making sure to mention the added responsibilities you have recently taken on with your new work situation. The answer may be as simple as a change in your diet, though it's best not to try to wait the problem out, nor is it a good idea to try to find your own remedy. If left untreated, your sleep disorder could become a major obstacle and create more stress in your life than you already have.

Perhaps before seeing your doctor, though, it might be sufficient to look at your diet and exercise routines. Sometimes a nice cup of herbal tea and a hot bath might be the ticket to helping you relax and feel ready for sleep.

ANXIETY

As we already discussed in the section on sleep, anxiety can find its way into the bedroom, waking you up in a panic that you haven't finished, or will not finish, an important project. Often, however, anxiety manifests itself in the conscious realm of our daily routines. For example, it can grip you when you are in the middle of doing something and find that you have more work than you initially thought. Anxiety, which often manifests itself in what's called a "panic attack," can result in rapid heartbeat, sweaty palms, difficulty breathing, and a feeling of being overwhelmed. It's rather common, though it needs to be treated by a physician if it becomes a more intense and recurring problem.

If you find yourself gripped with anxiety and it is physically taking you over, take a break. Walk away from the desk or step away from the task and get some air or splash some water on your face. Try to get to a place where you can be alone to look rationally at whatever is creating your stress. Make lists if you feel overwhelmed. If you still feel you have an insurmountable amount of things to do, tell your supervisor before things get out of hand and you are left handing in unfinished work on your deadline.

If you find that anxiety is taking over and crippling you in your work environment, and your being away from your job is more a rule than an exception, go to your physician and tell her in detail what your symptoms are and what, in particular, is causing you such physical and emotional stress. If panic attacks are recurring, you may have to cut yourself a break and shed off some of the burden you've taken on. It's often difficult to accept that we can't do it all, but remember that you come before any job you've set out to do and, more importantly, keep in mind that you're only human. Don't take on too much; learn sometimes to say "no!"

TAKE CONTROL MANAGING STRESS

There are any number of ways to alleviate stress—from playing a game of basketball to seeking professional counseling. No matter how you choose to alleviate stress, it's important you deal with it in a positive and productive manner. Ignoring signs of stress will only make matters worse in the long run.

MAKE LISTS

Did you ever meet anyone who was a compulsive list-maker? It may seem a little bizarre at first, but the person is usually pretty organized and less stressed, especially fresh after completing a "to-do list." Making lists is actually a very effective way of getting a grip on what needs to get done. Not only is it a means of keeping track of your obligations, deadlines, and priorities, it's a visual means of checking to see if everything you've piled on your plate is doable. Checking off what you've completed on a "to-do list" gives you a feeling of satisfaction and accomplishment, fueling you to take on the next task with which you will need to grapple.

If you're only at the beginning stages of juggling multiple jobs, make a list of all other priorities that you have, listing them in the order in which they matter to you. Keep this list handy at all times, referring to it when things begin to get chaotic in your life. This will probably be one of the most important lists you will ever write; it'll help you maintain clarity when your life becomes a jumble of responsibilities. It'll keep you on top of what you need to keep from losing sight of, whether it is your dog, your girlfriend, your husband, or your mom.

EXERCISE

Exercise is probably the most inexpensive yet most effective means of combating stress in your life. While allowing you to rid yourself of the tensions of the day, it helps restore your vibrancy by giving you more energy. Exercise will keep you from burning out as quickly, both physically and mentally. Tests have shown that exercise counteracts emotional and physical depression. The literal meaning of depression is a low level of activity. Now, you're probably thinking "that's the last thing I'm suffering from. I have too much activity going on." Though you may be running around during your actual day-to-day activities, your body may be resisting the movement and slowing down internally.

It's always a good idea to maintain an exercise regimen, but it's especially important for those of us who find ourselves working constantly and find less time for outdoor activities and other hobbies that may have once kept us in tip-top physical shape. It may seem almost counterintuitive to cut, let's say, an hour from our sleep so we can wake up for a morning jog because we are working so hard, but in reality that hour of exercise, even if it's a brisk walk, is much more useful than an hour's worth of snoozing. You don't even need to join a gym. Even minimal exercise will get you going in the morning. Try sit-ups, push-ups, jumping rope, jogging or walking, pull-ups (invest in a pull-up bar to hang in the door frame), or just take the stairs instead of the elevator in the office.

DIET

Make it a point to keep your diet a healthy one, full of vitamins and nutrients. Not to sound like your mother, but eat your fruits and vegetables! And don't neglect the other food groups either. Food is an important source of energy, especially at a time when you're working for two, so don't start eating for two but do keep your energy level high with lots of fresh, healthy foods.

And never make alcohol a combatant for stress. It's one thing to have a social drink with a colleague or friend, or a glass of wine with your dinner, but if you find yourself coming home and releasing tension by drinking alcohol, or if you're drinking often and by yourself, stop. But if you cannot stop by yourself, seek professional help. Drinking is not a release for stress.

HOBBIES AND SPORTS

Playing sports can be more enjoyable than going to the gym or going for a run, and it's important to try to keep such activities a constant in our lives and not immediately cut them out because we think they should not be a priority. Playing on an intramural soccer team with a bunch of friends may seem silly and meaningless on the surface when compared with some important presentation you have coming up next week, but it's actually important for two reasons. First, it's a source of exercise that's necessary to stay focused and efficient with the work you do, whatever it may be—be it buying and selling stocks or acting on Broadway. Second, it's an important source of social interaction at a time when you're finding it hard to squeeze in all the people you care about into your compressed and limited schedule. As you can see, joining a league of some sort with friends would be an ideal way of killing two birds with one stone, and combining both your social hour and your work-out hour into one neat package.

If sports are not your thing, try to maintain some sort of exercise in your schedule. That cannot be stressed enough! There are other hobbies you may have that you notice may be affected, and most often neglected, due to your increased workload. Whatever your hobby is—be it reading, playing an instrument, or gossiping on the phone—find time for it! Don't give up the simple things from which you get enjoyment. And again, these things may seem less important than some of the important work projects that you have going on, but you should realize that you need to relax to release stress. The only way to do that is to maintain a life outside of work, or else you will burn out.

PAMPER YOURSELF

Homeopathic oils, candles, scents—especially aromatherapeutic ones—are wonderful and have shown an improvement in people's moods and energy levels. Aromatherapy stores have been opening up all over the country in the past couple of years, and all the women's and men's magazines cannot get enough of them. It's no wonder, because they do work. Stores like The Gap have even tapped into the trend, coming up with candles as well as perfumes and aftershaves with names like "grass" (which doesn't actually smell like cut grass, but does indeed have a calming, earthy scent). The Body Shop and Bath and Body Works are more stores which also have fun soaps and bath oils and powders that are just absolutely luxurious! It's all about pampering yourself and taking time to indulge your senses, after neglecting them during a hard day's work.

Why not rub some tingly, mint body lotion on your aching feet, or shower using tingly shampoo that feels like getting a massage? But certainly, get the real thing, if you can. Our overworked generation has needed release from stress and The Great American Backrub, a chain of massage parlors, has been established. In short, make use of what's out there and just remember to make yourself feel good in a healthy way, every now and then. It'll give you a perk.

THERAPY

Sometimes we need to have someone help us manage our stress before it becomes unbearable. It's never a bad idea to make use of professionals who are certified and trained to help us combat dangerous levels of stress in our lives. In several sections of this chapter, we have discussed the idea of seeking the advice and counsel of a medical doctor in relieving some of the physical symptoms of stress.

In this particular section we will be discussing doctors and therapists who are trained in helping people combat the mental and emotional challenges of stressful life-styles. It is hoped you will find that these options can be a helpful and mature way to cope with the challenges you hope to meet.

We all know the stereotypes about therapists and, even worse, about people who seek therapy. We are a culture that refers to psychologists as "shrinks," not seeing the contradiction, when in fact people often broaden their minds and capabilities from seeking counseling, rather than "shrinking" them. When dealing with issues of stress and the overwhelming sensation that comes over many of us during stressful, difficult times, we need to go to others for advice, support, or sometimes just to be heard. Some people seek support from friends, elders, family, whereas others go to therapists or counselors. There are pros and cons to both options.

Sometimes it is nicer to go to a friend, our brother or sister, or even our moms and dads for help in learning to maintain some order in our lives that have become so hectic and stressful. These people generally know us and our tendencies to worry too much or too little. They know about the different elements in our lives, things that are going on simultaneously, causing much of our anxiety after having taken on another job. Most important, these people are also close to us, and we know they care.

That's not to say that there are no risks to going to people we know for help or advice. Often we create rifts with the people in our lives when we put too much of our worries and problems on their shoulders. Although our elders often have life experience that cannot be underestimated, most of our friends, family members, and spouses, unlike therapists, are not equipped to give the guidance we need in stressful times, simply because they are not trained to give such advice.

The greatest advantage to seeking therapy is the formality in the relationship between you and the therapist. This person is doing his or her job—something for which she is trained and is experienced in. You don't have to feel like you're burdening this person with your problems and worries. You don't have to take her advice if you don't agree with it, and she won't take it to heart. And most importantly, you will learn stress management skills that have proven successful for many other people who may have had similar experiences as the ones you are dealing with today.

If you work for a firm or company, find out from the human resources department about personal development courses that may be offered. Often, corporations have stress-management-skill courses that could be very inexpensive, if not free. If your company or employer does not offer such courses, find out through your insurance carrier about seeking therapy through insurance. If you have an HMO, or managed care, the cost is usually the same as seeking treatment from a medical practitioner, depending on what your copay is. If your insurance does not offer such assistance, most psychologists offer treatment on a sliding-scale basis, taking into account what your income is and basing their fee on what is affordable.

Whatever you do, make your decision based on what you're comfortable with, not what you assume people will think. Your boss will never know if you elect to seek counseling through work, because such matters are kept strictly confidential. Your friends and family do not need to know unless you want them to. Those you care about will probably be better off interacting with a happier, healthier you.

If you feel the need to seek professional counseling to alleviate stress brought on by a second job, you might want to reconsider whether to hold on to the job. If the second job is making you truly unhappy, then the responsibilities of your new job may not be worth it in the long run. However, if you must hold on to the second job for, say, financial reasons, although you're feeling overwhelmed by stress, then by all means professional assistance may prove helpful.

LAST BUT NOT LEAST

Remember just to take time out and do nothing. Go for a walk, go see a light movie, or just call or write a letter to a friend you've been meaning to contact. You'd be surprised at how this can help alleviate stress. More often than not, it's just what the doctor ordered!

Here are two exercises that will help you manage stress. Complete each exercise honestly.

EXERCISE 1

The following is a list of general statements. Answer "yes" or "no" to all nineteen statements, and then read the instructions that follow.

1. I know my long-term goals.
2. I know my short-term goals.
3. I base my actions on my goals.
4. I don't lose sight of my goals.
5. My goals are achievable.
6. I plan my time and activities.
7. I keep track of appointments.
8. My activities don't overlap.
9. I am on time for engagements.
10. I have adequate time for my various activities.
11. I keep track of my progress and achievements.
12. I am organized.
13. My weight is stable.
14. I am usually patient and calm.
15. I'm in good general health.
16. My friends and family support my goals and do not complain.
17. I enjoy what I do.
18. I look forward to going to work.
19. I have adequate time for myself.

If you answered no to three or more of the twenty statements, you should reevaluate your health, schedule, and perhaps your second job. Go over the statements to which you answered "no" and think what you would have to do to change the answer to "yes." Go over these with a close friend or spouse.

If you have a hard time figuring out what changes and improvements to make, write a brief paragraph about the statements to which you answered "no," explaining why you feel that way. Read it over. This is an effective exercise in learning how to listen to yourself.

EXERCISE 2

Write a page or two responding to each of the following statements:

> What makes me the happiest during my week long schedule is...
> I don't have enough time to...
> I find that I work exceptionally well on the days when...
> When I am not working, I usually...
> What I look most forward to is...

Read over your essay and underline the things in your life that cause the most distress. Highlight the things that help alleviate some of your stress, and find time in your schedule to incorporate these activities into your lifestyle so you can have more positive energy.

Having a second job doesn't have to mean you no longer have a life or that you will inevitably feel stress. Indeed, many individuals around the country balance their first and second jobs quite nicely. By following the guidelines outlined in this chapter, you'll be able to enjoy the perks of having a second job.

◆ ◆ ◆

It's Not Just in the Numbers: Alex's Story

Alex is a twenty-five-year-old accountant who lives in New York City. While growing up, he played many instruments in school bands, including the violin and the piano. As he went into his teenage years, he realized that music caught the attention of girls, so he soon taught himself how to play the guitar and got himself a set of keyboards. Throughout his four years in college, he was in several rock-and-roll bands and played at campus parties. His dream was to someday become a musician and songwriter.

Upon graduation, Alex learned that it would be difficult for him to move out of his parents' home and live on his own while struggling as an aspiring musician. He had to weigh the pros and cons of making a career decision. "I really don't think I have that starving-artist mentality," he laughs. "I can't go each day wondering if I can pay the rent, the electricity bill, the phone bill. I just couldn't wholly devote my life to music that way."

But Alex's day job in an accounting firm didn't afford him many creative outlets. Soon, he was left wondering if in the end he was losing out by trying to live a secure life. In short, Alex was feeling frustrated at his day job because of his lack of creative opportunities. "Number crunching all day long drives me crazy! I was constantly hearing music in my head and coming up with crazy riffs that I wasn't doing anything with. I rarely have the energy or the time to play music the way I want to. I can't start a band because my hours are so hectic and unpredictable. And I really almost gave up and came close to selling my equipment that first year out of school."

For nearly a year, Alex remained dedicated to his job and tried not to think back to the part of his life that he had abandoned. But he still found himself unfulfilled. One day he picked up his guitar and started playing again. He also later sat down at his keyboard and wrote a song. Getting back into the swing of his instruments and music helped him to feel less tense and more content.

"Playing music is what I love to do. I don't even really like playing other people's music. When I feel something, I take that energy and turn it into a song," he explains. "It's really soothing. And when I don't do it, I get really tense. But when I lose myself in it and get so absorbed in it, I just begin to feel like myself."

When he came to the realization that he couldn't give up his music, he began to look at the different options he had. Once again, he considered leaving his day job to try to establish a career in the music industry. But he soon decided that playing with a band wasn't really what he wanted, and the kind of music he liked to play wasn't even suitable for a band. He was clearly not interested in giving up a steady paycheck and health benefits with which his accounting job provided him. So he began looking around and asking questions. "It was really strange to see that I had so many contacts that I wasn't aware of. I was home for the holidays and my family had company over, and I started talking to my cousin. He's in his second year at art school studying film and he gave me a really great idea," he reflects. "When those kids enter their student films in film festivals and contests, they can't just stick in a U2 song; those songs are copyrighted, the bands are supposed to get paid. It gets really complicated." So Alex decided to start writing film scores for student films. "Hey, it's a reason to do what I love. And it's a chance to get heard!"

Today, Alex is actively pursuing his dreams of playing music, seeking film students interested in the kind of music he likes to write. He still has his job in accounting and believes that what he's doing on the side does not detract from his job performance. "In fact," he says in defense, "I think I'm much more focused. My days don't seem so dreary anymore. I mean, who knows, I may never make it as a musician, but I don't have to learn the hard way, and I'm simply doing what I love to do. In the end, even if nothing comes of it for me, I can have someone's reel and say, 'hey, I wrote the music to this' and I don't care if it's not a big Hollywood blockbuster."

Alex has stayed at his accounting job and has since been promoted. He still writes and plays music, often composing scores for student films. Though he has less free time than before, he feels more content, with a well-paying job and a hobby on the side that could someday prove to be his dream come true, professionally. He works hard to make sure that his two jobs do not overlap. He keeps an accurate record of what he has to do each day. He creates his list of things to do the night before, just before he goes to bed. He then adds to the list, if needed, during breakfast. As an accountant, he was trained to be well-organized. Now, as he's begun to pursue his musical interests, he's using his organizational training a great deal. "I have to be well-organized if I'm going to make a go of my interest in music. I have to know where to be and at what time if I'm going to get some work with my music. Because I'm so busy at my day job, I do all my thinking about my music at night or in the morning. Organization and focus are my new buzz words. Without them I'd be a mess at both jobs."

Having two jobs gives Alex the opportunity to pursue something that would not have provided a secure life-style. He doesn't worry about money, and actually has begun to make a little extra supplemental income. He hopes that what now is more of a hobby than a job could be a springboard to something bigger, so that he may someday have the career he truly wants, not just a job that pays the bills. "Right now I feel like I'm paying my dues. I have hardly any time to myself," he explains. "I still don't spend as much time on music as I'd like to, since I'm at my job for at least eight hours every day. I'm hoping that eventually I can prove myself, get a break, and be able to really dedicate myself to writing music."

◆ ◆ ◆

Working Out: Lynn's Story

Lynn is a twenty-seven-year-old hairstylist. When she was in high school she began taking classes offered by her school for students who did not plan to go to college. She prepared for employment upon graduation and was offered a job soon after she finished school. She first began by shampooing hair and sweeping the floor, watching the other stylists and learning different techniques of cutting hair.

Soon enough, Lynn began cutting hair and, for the most part, she enjoyed her job. "It's kind of fun. You meet a lot of people, and the money's not bad, especially after you establish a good clientele and get repeat business," she said. "It's nice to know that people are happy with the work you do. The tips are usually pretty good, too." But a few years later, Lynn began reconsidering her career options after working as a hairdresser. "I never considered going to college because my parents couldn't afford it, and I was never an exceptional student," she explains. "But I talk to so many of my friends from high school and many of them were not exactly honor students either, and a lot of them did end up going to college. I guess I feel like I missed out and didn't really have that experience to see if there's something I may be really good at." Lynn doesn't regret having made the decision to become a hairdresser and rather enjoys what she does. "I like what I do and I know I'm good at it. I just know there's more for me out there."

Money is the one issue that kept Lynn from going to college. After a great deal of thought, she decided to take some general studies classes at a nearby community college. Money was still an issue, but Lynn was determined to work this detail out. "I wasn't going to let money keep me from exploring what my options are this time around," she said. "I know that was a huge obstacle for me when I was younger, so I never considered going to college, and that's one of the reasons I didn't excel in school. I want it to be different this time."

Lynn made the decision to take a night job and save her money to take a few night courses. She knew it would be difficult, but was convinced that in the end her efforts would pay off. "I knew I'd be working really hard, with a day job and then a night job. I also knew I really wouldn't see any of the money, since I'd be spending it on school. I went back and forth with my decision but finally said 'I've really got to give it a shot.'" And so she looked at her skills and capabilities, making sure to read the classifieds daily. She decided that with her qualifications, the best and quickest way she could make extra money was by bartending.

"Bartending is difficult. It's a nice way to meet people, but it's really exhausting, especially working weekend nights when I know all my friends are out having fun, sitting on the other side of a bar somewhere." But Lynn saw the upside of her second job as well. "I learned how to make a lot of drinks!" she laughs. "And it's a good chance to learn what other people do and what makes them happy. And that's exactly why I've decided to make this change for myself—to go to college—to find out what makes me happy." Lynn also manages to make a good amount of money from tips and pay. Her savings have amounted to enough to pay for a few college courses. And she's consistent in putting away a good portion of her pay from her day job as well. "It's hard. I have so few hours to myself and I know that when I begin classes I'm going to have even fewer. I'm often scared and then excited, but I know in my heart that I'm doing the right thing, and I'm glad that I'm doing it all by myself."

While Lynn works at her two jobs, she often goes through the catalog of offered classes and thinks about the type of subjects she'd like to explore. "I look forward to what awaits me. And during the days when I feel exhausted and ready to give up, it gives me that extra push, that little extra energy that I need to make it through the rest of the evening," she explains. "I also want to try to find some kind of focus, try to figure what I'd like to study before registering."

Lynn has never regretted her decision to go back to school. But she didn't anticipate what would come along with her new life—stress brought on by doing too much at once. To alleviate the stress, she realized she had to get more active physically. In high school she had been on her school's basketball and track teams. She decided that basketball was out but that if she got up an hour earlier three or four mornings a week she could jog before she headed to college and her jobs. "I realized that it would add yet another item to my already overwhelming list of things to do, but I had to do something. I tell you, it was the best adjustment to my schedule I've made since going back to school. And a nice by-product of my jogging is I've lost more than ten pounds!"

Lynn's rethinking the career decision she made long ago is not uncommon. But she is different from most people in her ability to overcome the obstacles in her way. Knowing that money is what ultimately ruled out what she secretly desired but never considered—going to college—she took the steps necessary to attain her goal. She still likes her job as a hairdresser and works as efficiently as ever. Her part-time job as a bartender affords her the freedom to save more money in a shorter amount of time than she could if she were holding down only one job. She works hard and is thrifty with money, keeping in mind that her long-term goals are worth all the effort. "It is very difficult, and I'm the first person to admit that it's usually not always that much fun. But as long as it pays off, I know it's worth it. I know college will afford me a lot of freedom to explore things I would otherwise not be able to do, and that alone I think will help me in the long run."

3

PERSONAL FINANCE
What to Do With the Extra Money You've Earned

In order to profit from the extra income you will earn while moonlighting, it is important to determine your financial goals. This chapter will illustrate how to develop a financial plan through careful budgeting. It will also focus on paying off debt, insurance needs, and taxes. These are all important areas of concern when determining your financial picture.

Everyone has different financial goals. Some want to pay off debt, and others want to save for a new home, retirement, or for their children's education. The following chapter will demonstrate how to invest your extra income from moonlighting.

MEETING SHORT-TERM GOALS

A second job provides added income which can be used to meet short-term financial goals like paying off credit-card debt, saving money for an exotic vacation, or making a down payment on a new home. No matter what your reason for needing this money, you must create a budget to aid you in meeting your short-term financial goals. Here's how:

Step 1: State clearly your reason for saving money; to pay off debt, for a new car, etc.

Step 2: List the cost of the item you're looking to purchase or the amount of the debt you're looking to pay off. Be as exact as possible as to the amount of money you'll need so you don't come up short when it comes time to meet costs.

Step 3: Create a separate savings account for the income from your part-time job. That way, you can keep your savings for your short-term goals separate from your other accounts and other current monthly expenses.

Step 4: Figure on paper how long it will take you to meet your short-term financial goals. For example, if you're looking to spend $500 on a vacation, how long will it take you, relying on the income from your part-time job, to save that amount? Keep track of each of your deposits. List them on paper so that you know you'll have the money when you need it.

Step 5: When the date comes to cover the expense or pay off the debt, withdraw the money and enjoy the rewards of your commitment to achieving your short-term goal.

Many of us are also looking to budget for long-term goals. You'll find the remaining portion of this chapter helpful in planning long-term goals.

DEVELOPING A BUDGET

A budget is a plan that helps you structure the amount of money that you spend over a given period of time. Some individuals budget their expenses on a weekly, monthly, and annual basis. A good place to begin is to review your expenditures from the previous three months, although reviewing the previous year is ideal. This will provide a foundation for your budget and allow you to plan for the future with your added income. It is true that if you commit your budget to paper you are well on your way to developing more disciplined spending habits.

To begin to develop your personal budget it is important to itemize your fixed expenses. *Fixed expenses* are those expenses that recur on a weekly, monthly, and annual basis. For example:

Weekly: food, childcare cost, transportation
Monthly: mortgage, rent, utilities, credit card, other loan repayments
Annual: taxes, insurance, savings

The second part of your budget covers variable expenses. Variable expenses are more difficult to predict because your variable expenses, such as travel, entertainment, and gifts, will change from one year to the next. Therefore, it is important to estimate what you plan on spending for those items and then allot it to your *budget*.

The *budget* is the first part of your financial outline. It gives you direction, and it will allow you to plan to meet your goals for the future. Financial planning is an ongoing process. It is never too soon, or too late, to begin. Whether you intend to moonlight for a few months or turn your moonlighting job into a full-time career, it is important to continue the process and revise your plan as your financial circumstances change. Without a plan, you run the risk of not meeting your expenses or your long-term financial objectives for savings and investments.

In order to determine whether your budget is on track or way off base, below are some financial guidelines:

Outstanding debt (not including your mortgage) should not exceed 20 percent of your annual income. To determine if your budget meets this criteria, list all of your outstanding bills (i.e., student loans, credit cards, auto loans, and any other lines of credit). If this figure exceeds 20 percent of your take-home pay, then it is imperative that you first begin to reduce this debt, particularly since the interest rate on credit cards may be very high.

Mortgage or rent expenditures should not exceed more than 30 percent of your annual take-home pay. This is a good rule of thumb.

Savings should be budgeted at approximately 10 percent of your annual take-home pay. You need to begin saving after you have paid off all of your outstanding debt.

PAYING OFF DEBT

In order to secure your financial future, it is imperative that you control the amount of debt you carry. This section will outline ways to reduce your debt and create better credit habits.

Let's begin by determining which creditors to pay off first. Your fixed expenses, as outlined in the financial worksheet, need to be paid first in order for you to live in your home or apartment. Once you have covered your fixed expenses, then you can reduce the debt on your higher interest-bearing loans.

If you have a savings account set aside, pay off your outstanding debt first. The rate of interest that you are paying on your credit cards, auto loans, and other loan repayments is more than you could expect to receive on your investments. For example, let's say you have a savings account in the amount of $1,000, earning a rate of interest of 5 percent, and you owe a credit card company $1,000, which carries an 18 percent interest rate. If you hold the savings account for the year, you will earn $50 and pay $180 in interest on the credit card. However, if you pay off the $1,000 credit card bill, you will save a net $130 in interest. Therefore, it makes good financial sense to pay off debt with savings.

If you do not have the financial resources to pay off your debt right away, there are several ways to gain control of your debt. To begin, you can consolidate your high interest-rate loans to lower interest-rate loans. For example, several credit card companies allow you to transfer your debt from your higher interest-rate accounts to a new, lower-rate account. However, be cognizant that the lower rate on your new account might only be for a short term and then it could revert back to a higher rate after the introductory period. Be wary of taking cash advances on your credit card. Most credit card companies are willing to negotiate the rate of interest since the credit card business is so competitive. Therefore, it might not even be necessary for you to transfer your credit card debt to a new company.

Contact your existing credit card company and ask to speak to one of the supervisors. Let the supervisor know that you have other credit cards that have a lower rate of interest and, in a very friendly, but firm, manner advise her that if your request to lower your rate of interest is not met, you will cancel your card. Most companies want to keep your business, so you will more than likely meet with good news.

The interest rate on other types of loans, such as auto

and personal lines of credit, are more difficult to negotiate. Therefore, it is important to try to shop for the best
rate at the time you make the loan.

INSURANCE NEEDS

Insurance is an essential part of health maintenance and a
satisfying lifestyle. This section deals with your insurance needs. We will review the different types of insurance—auto, home, renters, life, medical, and disability—
and help you determine how much protection you should
have.

Insurance is an integral part of your financial plan as it
can protect you and your family against financial ruin. If
your employer offers an insurance plan, try to maximize
it. Most employers offer their full-time employees health
insurance and sometimes some life insurance. Often,
they will cover the cost of the insurance or share the cost
with you. This is a tremendous savings over attempting to
purchase these types of insurance on your own. However,
if moonlighting is your way of supplementing your insurance needs, it helps to be familiar with the various forms.

Life Insurance   If you are supporting a family or have
other financial obligations, it is important to insure yourself. In the event of your death, the insurance policy's
benefit would be able to fill the financial void. Although
this subject is one that many of us do not like to think
about, it is important to plan for our survivors. Basically,
there are two types of life insurance: *term insurance* and
permanent insurance.

Term Insurance   This is often the least expensive for the
amount of coverage. You can purchase it for a specified

period of time, hence its name. For example, you can purchase a term insurance policy and as long as you pay the premiums, you are covered. In the event of your death, your beneficiary will receive the death benefit.

Permanent Insurance   This differs from term insurance because you build up a reserve in the policy, commonly known as "cash value," and would be paid during a lifetime, should the insured discontinue premium payments. Permanent insurance is designed to provide protection for the life of the insured. Some of these policies have fixed rates of interest, and others allow you to invest the funds in variable accounts where the performance will be linked to the underlying investments.

Health Insurance   Everyone should have medical insurance. If you are employed full-time, your employer may offer you health insurance. These plans vary widely. Therefore, it would be wise to meet with your employer's insurance coordinator to understand your options. If you leave your job, and your company has over twenty employees, your employer is obligated to offer you medical insurance for eighteen months. You will cover the cost of the insurance and, oftentimes, they can require that you pay 102 percent of the cost. For example, if your health insurance cost is $100 per month, they will charge you $102 per month to continue the plan. This is still less than you would pay if you attempted to purchase a policy on your own. Such a policy could cost you as much as $450 per month. It is beneficial to shop around with different insurance companies because the rates will vary.

Automobile Insurance   Automobile insurance is required in most states. There are basically two types of coverage: *auto liability* coverage and *property damage.*

Liability insurance protects you in case you are in an

accident where someone is injured and you are held responsible. *Property damage* insurance will cover your automobile for any physical damage resulting from an accident. Requirements for automobile insurance differ from state to state. Therefore, you can inquire with a specific agent in your state, or contact your state insurance department.

Home Owners or Renters Insurance   Home Owners insurance is required by most lenders. Home owners insurance will provide coverage to rebuild or repair your home in the event of theft, flood, fire, or a natural disaster. It will also cover the contents of the home up to a specified amount. Renters insurance will cover the contents of your home.

Disability Insurance   Disability insurance will pay you a portion of your income in the event of sickness or injury. Most employers offer some coverage for long-term disability. Long-term disability typically becomes effective six months after one is sick or injured.

INCOME TAXES

The extra income that you are earning from your moonlighting could move you into a new tax bracket. If your employer is not withholding taxes from your paycheck, you will want to estimate how much additional tax you owe at the end of the year. Typically, financial advisors recommend withholding one-third of your income for the additional taxes owed. You could set up a savings account for your tax bill in order to ensure that the money is there when it is owed. The tax code is constantly changing, which makes it more difficult to prepare your own taxes. Professional tax preparation through a certified public accountant (CPA) can save you money in the long run. They can point out some of the new tax laws and how they might impact on your personal tax return. For example, if you are a freelance writer you might not be aware that the cost of a new computer you purchased can be deducted on your taxes.

If you would like to find a CPA to work with on your taxes, ask your friends, relatives, or colleagues for referrals. Most accountants will allow you to interview them over the phone. It is best to hire a CPA who specializes in individual tax returns. It is also a good idea to discuss the fee they will charge for the preparation of your tax return. You can expect to pay approximately $250 for a simple return or as much as $1,000 for a more complicated tax return. If you are computer literate, you might be able to prepare your taxes on one of the many tax programs available on the market today.

INVESTING FOR YOUR FUTURE

Investing means putting your money to work in order to earn more money. The added income that you earn from your part-time employment will help you begin a savings and investment plan, or add to the one already in place. But first you need to decide if investing is for you.

Your first priority is to make sure that you have covered your fixed living expenses. In addition, you want to pay off your high-interest debt as discussed earlier in this chapter. And last, but not least, reserve some of your current income for entertainment. Although saving and investing are important, it is good to be able to enjoy spending some of the extra income on yourself.

Once you decide you would like to start saving a

portion of your income, then it is important to determine your financial goals. Are you saving for a new home, a college education, or for retirement? How much can you afford to invest? And, how much should you invest? Where do you invest your money? This chapter will outline some of the fundamentals of saving and investing. In addition, it will give an overview of the various types of retirement savings plans available.

BANK ACCOUNTS

Bank accounts and other types of money-market savings accounts are the foundation of a good investment plan. They offer you liquidity and a high degree of safety. You can easily establish an account through a bank.

Savings in these accounts should equal at least three months worth of your expenses. This will provide you with some reserve in case you change or lose your employment.

The banking industry is very competitive. Some banks will offer you free checking accounts with some minimum balance requirements. Typically, they offer free checking if your combined balance is over $1,000 in checking, savings, and money market accounts.

You will want to open your account with a bank that is FDIC (Federal Deposit Insurance Corporation) insured. This insurance provides you with protection of up to $100,000 on deposits. In the event the bank fails, your deposits are backed by the federal government.

It is worth shopping around for a bank that will accommodate your personal needs. For example, it is important for you to feel comfortable with the bank when you walk in the door. Do they give you personal attention?

Are they willing to take the time to describe the different types of accounts available to you? You want to have a good relationship with your bank. Although banks can offer all types of investments, however, you are probably better off seeking the advice elsewhere, as we will discuss further in this chapter.

There are three basic investment categories: cash, stocks, and bonds. Let's begin by developing a foundation with cash for your investment portfolio.

STOCKS

Investing in stocks means you share in the ownership of a company. Or, as stockbrokers say, you have *equity* in the company. There are over 9,000 public companies. You can purchase shares of a company individually, or invest in a stock mutual fund, which we will discuss later in this chapter.

Some companies will pay you a dividend in order to encourage you to invest. The dividend is a portion of the earnings from your investment in the stock. It is taxable in the year in which it is earned, even if you reinvest the dividend into additional shares in the company. There are two different classes of stock ownership: *common* and *preferred*.

Common stockholders share in the profitability, or unprofitability, of the company in which they have invested. *Preferred* shareholders, on the other hand, earn a fixed dividend, and they are paid prior to common stockholders. Preferred stockholders have less risk than the common stockholder since they receive their dividends first. However, if the company has tremendous growth, the common stockholder will earn more from the increase in the value of the stock.

Some stocks are designed to pay high dividends and they are referred to as *income stocks*. Utilities and other large capitalization corporations are examples of this type of stocks. Income stocks appeal to those who are interested in generating current income from their investments.

Growth stocks do not typically pay dividends. They reinvest all of their earnings back into the company. If you are investing for the long term and are not looking for immediate income, then growth stocks will provide greater total return. You will want to monitor your investments as there are fluctuations in the market. Most investors are in for the long term. However, this does not mean that you purchase stocks and stick them in a drawer and don't look at them for twenty years. You need to play an active role with your investments in order to make sure that the performance is keeping pace with the major indices (i.e., *Standard & Poor's 500 Index*).

You probably hear on the nightly news reports that the *stock market* was up or down on a given day. This is just an indication of how the average stock price fared for the day. For example, we often hear references to the fluctuation of the Dow Jones. The Dow Jones Industrial Average is an average, or an index, of thirty large companies, which include McDonalds, Boeing, and AT&T. Another index that is commonly referred to is the *Standard & Poor's Index* of the top 500 common stocks. The price fluctuation of these two major indices gives you an overview of the performance of the market on a given day. Daily closing prices of most stocks can be found in your local paper and in the *Wall Street Journal*.

Value Line is a stock-rating service that publishes weekly reports on publicly traded corporations. They rate companies on their timeliness and safety. The reports are very detailed, listing the revenues, earnings, projected returns, dividend history, and a brief narrative on the company. *Value Line* reports are available at your local library. You can also subscribe to *Value Line* by contacting them by phone (1-800-833-0046) or reaching them on the Internet (*www.valueline.com*).

BONDS

When you purchase a bond, you are making a loan to a corporation, to a municipality, or to the federal government. These entities have agreed to pay you a fixed rate of interest for a specified period of time. Ownership in a bond is referred to as a *debt* security, which is different from the *equity* security we discussed in stock ownership.

Bonds are issued in increments of $1,000, and they can be purchased either individually or through a bond mutual fund. Bonds are issued for a specified period of time, or maturity period. However, if you purchase an individual bond, you are not obligated to hold the bond until maturity.

Bonds are bought and sold every day. Therefore, bonds are a very liquid investment. In addition, the bond market is three times the size of the stock market. Since bonds provide such a high degree of safety, they attract many investors. There are four different types of bonds: corporate, municipal, treasury, and agency.

Corporate bonds are issued by a corporation, and they are backed by the full faith and credit of the corporation. Moody's and Standard & Poor's are two credit-rating agencies that rate the ability of the corporation to repay the interest and the principal of the loan. They rate bonds from the highest degree of safety to the lowest: AAA, AA, A, BBB, BB, etc. If you are purchasing individual corporate bonds, you will want to buy bonds that are investment grade. Investment grade bonds are rated BBB or higher. These bonds will provide you with greater safety. The *Wall Street Journal* randomly lists the prices and yields for some of the more frequently traded corporate bonds.

Municipal bonds are issued by state and local governments. There are two types of municipal bonds: general obligation and revenue bonds. *General obligation* bonds are backed by the full faith and credit of the issuer. They are the obligation of the taxpaying community. School bonds and highway bonds are a couple of examples of general obligation bonds. *Revenue* bonds are backed by the earning capacity of the project. Some states and cities issue revenue bonds to construct such products as stadiums, airports, or hospitals.

The interest from municipal bonds is both federal and state tax-free if you purchase bonds in the state in which you reside. Municipal bonds are a very attractive investment for those individuals in a high tax bracket since the interest is tax-free. The *Wall Street Journal* provides a brief list of municipal bonds in order to give an indication of pricing and yield.

Treasury bonds, notes, and *bills* are issued by the federal government. They are backed by the full faith and credit of the American taxpayers. Therefore, these bonds have the highest credit quality. The interest on treasury bonds is state tax-free but federally taxable. Treasury bills are short-term securities that are issued for less than one year. Treasury notes are intermediate term-2–10 years. And treasury bonds are longer-term investments, 10–30 years.

Agency bonds are issued by state and federal agencies. They are backed by the specific agency that issues the bonds and therefore are not a direct obligation of the federal government, like the treasury bonds discussed above. The most commonly known agency is GNMA, which is the federally guaranteed, mortgage-backed bonds. Treasury and agency prices and yields are listed in the *Wall Street Journal* and in most local newspapers.

You can also purchase all types of bonds through a mutual fund. There are mutual funds that invest only in corporate bonds, municipal bonds, treasury bonds, or agency bonds.

Most of these funds can be purchased with a minimum investment of $250, and you can make subsequent purchases to the fund for as little as $25–$100. Mutual funds will be discussed in more detail in the next section.

MUTUAL FUNDS

Mutual funds allow you to pool your money with other investors with common goals and have a professional manage the funds on your behalf. Based on your risk tolerance and investment goals, you can select a mutual fund that is designed to meet your objectives.

There are over 7,500 mutual funds available today. Before you make an investment make sure you have read through the prospectus that is issued by the mutual fund. This informative document outlines the types of securities that the money manager can purchase in the fund, and the annual costs the fund will charge your account to manage the money.

You can invest in stock funds, bond funds, or sector

funds, targeting a specific area of the economy. Mutual funds offer investors the following benefits:

Diversification of Assets Mutual funds typically own between 30 and 100 different stock or bond positions. This diversification gives the individual greater safety versus owning one or two stocks or bonds.

Professional Money Management The money managers on the specific funds are experts in their field. Their expertise in money management lends safety to your investment.

Reinvestment Options You have the ability to reinvest the dividends from the fund back into additional shares of the fund.

Income Options Mutual funds offer a variety of ways of receiving your income distributions. You can take the income monthly, quarterly, or annually.

Low Buy-In Cost You can start a mutual fund with an investment of between $100 and $3,000. Once you have established your account, you can purchase additional shares for as little as $25–$100. Therefore, mutual funds are very accessible to the first-time investor.

Liquidity Mutual funds can be sold on a daily basis by contacting the fund directly. Many of the funds offer telephone redemptions. Some funds offer a feature called wire redemption. This allows you to sell shares in your fund and have the proceeds wired to your bank account. This feature needs to be set up when you establish the account.

Transfer Within Fund Family Most mutual fund companies manage many different mutual funds within the same fund group. Therefore, they allow their investors to transfer within the same fund group without a charge. If your financial circumstances change, or if the economy changes, you may want to transfer from one fund to another.

Mutual funds can be purchased through a stockbroker or on your own. If you buy a fund through a broker, you will probably pay a load or a *commission*. This *commission* is paid to the broker in order for them to monitor the investment on your behalf.

There are front-end load mutual funds and back-end load mutual funds. If you purchase a fund that has a front-end load, this means that the fee is taken from the investment prior to the money being invested. And a back-end load fund charges its fee, or contingent-deferred sales charge, if you surrender the fund prior to the specified number of years outlined in the prospectus.

No-load funds can be purchased by contacting the specific mutual-fund company. They will not be able to give you advice on your investment or monitor the fund for you. Therefore, if you are not a very savvy investor and do not have time to monitor your investment, then it probably makes sense to seek the advice of a broker. If you purchase a no-load fund, this does not mean that there are no fees. All mutual funds charge an annual fee or a management fee. Typically, management fees are between 0.5 and 1.0 percent per year, depending on the fund.

Many investors purchase mutual funds through dollar-cost averaging. This allows the investor to make an initial investment in a fund and then make subsequent purchases into the same fund each month, for example. Let's say you had $300 to invest. The mutual fund that you wanted to buy was selling for $10 per share. If you invest all $300 at once you will purchase thirty shares of the fund. However, as you are aware, the stock market is volatile and prices fluctuate. Dollar-cost averaging allows you to take advantage of the volatility in the market. Now, let's say you decided to invest your $300 in three equal purchases over the next three months. In the first month you invest your $100, and the price of the fund is $10 per share and you have ten shares. In the second month, you invest your $100, and the price of the fund has dropped considerably to $5 per share and you are able to purchase twenty shares. In the third month you invest your $100, and the price has come back to $10 per share and you purchase ten additional shares. Now, you own forty shares at a price of $10, or $400, which is a total return of 33⅓ percent. Contrast this scenario with the example of the investor making one investment of $300. The price fluctuated while the investor owned the fund. However, he did not take advantage of the price swings. Since we know the stock market will fluctuate, dollar-cost averaging allows the investor to purchase more shares over time.

Morningstar is a mutual-fund-rating service. That groups mutual funds according to their sector of the economy. They rank funds on a star system from one star to five star (five star being the best in their sector). Morningstar provides a brief analysis of the fund with some of the following information: dividend history, management changes, total return performance, price fluctuations, and expenses. Their reports are available at your local library. You can subscribe to the service by calling 1-800-735-0700. They can also be reached on the Internet (*www.morningstar.net*).

Mutual funds are a terrific investment for first-time investors. They provide you with the benefit of safety through diversification in assets, with a very low initial investment. You have the opportunity to own many stocks or bonds that you might not be able to afford to purchase on an individual basis.

INVESTING FOR YOUR RETIREMENT

One of the reasons that you might be investing your additional income is for retirement. Social Security and apension fund will provide some of the income you will need in retirement. Typically, the average retiree will replace 60 percent of his or her income from Social Security and pensions. Therefore, it is necessary for you to save and invest in a retirement account to replace the other 40 percent of the income you had earned while working.

Many employers offer qualified retirement plans, (although it is legal for an employer not to offer one at all). There are many different types of plans that are employer-sponsored, and others that you as the employee control. One of the tremendous benefits of qualified retirement plans is that the earnings are tax-deferred. As a condition of participating in the plan, you must leave the funds invested until age fifty-nine and a half. At that point in time you will pay taxes on the earnings in the plan as ordinary income. If you chose to withdraw the prior to age fifty-nine and a half, you will pay a 10 percent Internal Revenue Service penalty, in addition to the taxes on the earnings.

These funds are designed to help replace your income in retirement. Therefore, it makes sense to allow them to grow and accumulate for that time. Let's begin by reviewing some of the plans available.

INDIVIDUAL RETIREMENT ACCOUNT (IRA)

There are three different types of IRA accounts: deductible, nondeductible, and the Roth IRA.

Deductible IRA   Anyone with earned income who is not covered by an employer-sponsored retirement plan is eligible for the $2,000 maximum tax-deductible contribution. For those participating in employer-sponsored retirement plans, the limits are: adjusted gross income of $30,000 or less will receive the full deduction; the amount of the deduction phases out with adjusted gross income between $30,000–$40,000.

Married Filing Jointly   You are eligible for the full tax deduction if a spouse is an active participant in an employer-sponsored retirement plan, with adjusted gross income of $50,000 or less. In addition, effective 1/1/98, individuals who are not active participants in retirement plans but with spouses who are active in retirement plans and have adjusted gross income of $150,000 or less can use the full tax deduction.

The tax deduction phases out with an adjusted gross income of $50,0001, $60,000 if a spouse is an active participant in an employer-sponsored retirement plan. And effective 1/1/98, the tax deduction phases out with an adjusted gross income of $150,000–$160,000 if you are not an active participant in a plan, but your spouse is active.

Withdrawals from IRA accounts prior to age fifty-nine and a half are subject to a 10 percent penalty. After age fifty-nine and a half the withdrawals are taxed as ordinary income. You must begin taking a minimum withdrawal by April 1st in the year after you turn seventy and a half. The minimum mandatory withdrawal figures are calculated based on the life expectancy of the individual. Individuals can invest their IRAs as they choose. You can invest in mutual funds, stocks, bonds, or real estate. Since these are retirement funds, it is best to invest somewhat conservatively (high quality stocks, bonds, or conservative equity or bond mutual funds).

Nondeductible IRA The maximum contribution to a nondeductible IRA is $2,000 per year. There are no adjusted gross-income limits since the contribution is nondeductible. The withdrawals from these accounts is still penalized by 10 percent if done prior to age fifty-nine and a half. And after age fifty-nine and a half, the income is taxed as ordinary income. Minimum withdrawals must also begin by April 1st of the year after the individual turns 70½.

Roth IRA This new IRA tax-advantaged-retirement plan came into effect with the Taxpayer Relief Act of 1997. The plan is named for Senator William V. Roth Jr., who has been a long-time advocate of increased tax incentives for retirement savings. Although the contributions to the Roth IRA are not tax-deductible, the earnings grow tax-deferred. Individuals can invest in the Roth IRA at any age, as long as your earned income is below $110,000, if filing as a single, and $150,000 if filing jointly. Allowed contributions phase out for those earning $95,000 filing as a single and $150,000 filing jointly. The maximum contribution to the plan is $2,000 per year.

If you have existing IRA accounts, you can convert them into a Roth IRA account if your adjusted gross income is $100,000 or less. However, the owner of the IRA must pay a one-time tax at their normal income tax rate when the conversion is made. One of the benefits of the Roth IRA is that the withdrawals are tax-free and penalty-free if the amount does not exceed the contribution. The account must have been open for at least five years, the owner must be at least fifty-nine and a half, and the withdrawal must be for a first-time home purchase (up to $10,000 withdrawal). There are no minimum-age withdrawal requirements. The account can grow tax-deferred until the owner's death.

Tax-deferred growth and a compounded return on your investment really add up over time. For example, this illustration shows the results of one individual's return on a $2,000 annual investment over the specified time periods and with the stated rates of return.

RATES OF RETURN

Years	8%	10%
10 years	$30,490	$34,141
20 years	$98,162	$126,557
30 years	$248,358	$376,723

The sooner you get started with your investment the longer it has to work for you. As they say, it is not timing the market or your investments, but instead it is time (years) in the market or in your investments.

SALARY REDUCTION RETIREMENT PLANS

401-K Plans   Although this plan usually applies to full-time workers, if your employer offers a salary reduction retirement savings plan it is important to maximize it. Some employers match your contributions up to a certain percentage. This is free money! Therefore, you should maximize your retirement savings in your 401-K plan first. This type of plan allows you to invest pretax income into a special account set up by your employer. For example, if you have earned income of $50,000 in a given year and you made pretax contributions to your 401-K of $5,000, your employer reports only $45,000 in earned income on your W–2 tax form. You do not pay taxes on the contribution or the earnings until you begin to withdraw from the plan. Withdrawals prior to age fifty-nine and a half are assessed a 10 percent IRS penalty. The preset limit for contributions to these plans for 1997 is $9,500. Some employers allow you to make after-tax contributions to your 401-K. The earnings from these contributions also grow tax-deferred.

403-B Plans   If you are employed by a nonprofit, tax-exempt organization—public schools, for example—they will offer you the opportunity to invest in a 403-B plan. As with the 401-K plan, you have the ability to make pretax and after-tax contributions. The preset limit on contributions is 20 percent of your salary, or up to a limit of $9,500. The caps on the 403-B and 401-K plans are increased annually to keep pace with the rate of inflation.

If your moonlighting business means you are self-employed, work with your professional tax advisor on setting up a Self-Employed Plan (SEP-IRA), or a Keogh account. A CPA will be able to guide you on how much you can invest into one of these tax-advantaged retirement plans. You might be able to put away more money for retirement than with one of the traditional IRA accounts we discussed earlier.

In review, it is essential to begin your savings and investment plan with a foundation of checking and money market accounts. These funds will provide you with a reserve in case of an emergency or a job change. Once you have established the foundation, you can begin to branch out with your investments by purchasing mutual funds, individual stocks, or individual bonds. The important thing is to get started now and put time on your side. The longer your time horizon for investing, the better your chances for increased returns. You work hard for your money, so why not pay yourself through setting up some investment accounts that will secure your financial future in retirement?

The following financial worksheet is a guideline to help you begin developing a budget. After you have completed your budget you will have a better handle on your personal finances.

MONTHLY FINANCIAL WORKSHEET

Income (From work or other income sources):

Salary (before tax), Income from other jobs (before tax), Investment Income (earnings, dividends, and interest—before tax), Other

Total Income Per Month:

Expenses (Cost of living per month):

Mortgage or Rent; Federal, State, Local, and FICA Taxes, Tax on investment income; Utilities (phone, electricity, gas); Groceries; Auto Loans; Auto Expenses (gas, etc.) Other: Loan Repayments; Insurance Premiums (life, health, disability, auto, medical, and homeowners); Public Transportation; Travel & Entertainment; Home Expenses (maintenance, furniture); Savings (401(k) contributions, etc.); Hobbies, Health Club Fees, etc.; Charitable Contributions; Clothing; Other Miscellaneous Expenses

Total Expenses Per Month:
Total Income:
Total Expenses:
Equals Net Monthly Income:

◆ ◆ ◆

Working to Balance the Budget: Carl's Story

Visa: $125. MasterCard: $60. Rent: $525. Car insurance: $250. Images of Carl's monthly bills floated about him, especially in the early-morning hours, even before his alarm went off, like clothes in a washing machine in the spin-cycle. There were mornings when he would wake up dizzy and out of breath, thinking of his mounting debt.

Carl had seen the TV commercials touting the pluses of second-home mortgages. But Carl didn't own a home. He was still renting his apartment in Indianapolis's northside. His credit-card companies were also constantly sending him letters telling him about their different loan programs. But—at 18 percent interest—he knew the terrors of such loans. Carl was at a loss. He knew he had to do something to gain control of his debt and of his quality of life—the bills, the weekend calls from collection agencies, were eating away at him emotionally.

As an actuary at a local insurance agency, Carl's hours at work were standard nine to five. He was usually home by 5:30, when he would then call friends to meet for dinner. Carl would often spend as much as $40 on a night out with his friends. Without realizing it, he was almost literally eating and drinking himself into debt. He would tell himself he liked to go out with friends because it was fun. But he also knew going out allowed him to avoid dealing with his bills.

One evening, when Carl was at his favorite restaurant with a college friend, he saw a sign in the restaurant's window saying it was hiring a new wait staff. The idea to apply for the position occurred to him, as he said, "...right there on the spot. Caroline's has always been a place I've gone to because the food's good and because it has excellent service. I've always gotten along well with the waiters and waitresses there, and many of them know me as a regular. If I got the job, I knew I would fit in right away."

Besides working with bright and interesting people, Carl also saw many other advantages to working in the restaurant. First and foremost, he saw it as a way to alleviate some of his debt. "I was talking to one of the waiters, telling him I was thinking of applying for a job there. He told me that he pulled in more than $150 a night from tips alone. Wow! That figure almost knocked me on the floor right there. After doing the numbers, I realized with that as added income I could pay off my debt—which at the time was in the low five figures—within the year. I also knew that if I got the job I wouldn't be out spending money, I would be out making it instead."

There was another, more emotional attachment Carl had for seeking a job at the restaurant, however. "My father managed a small restaurant in the town I grew up in. But I saw how hard my dad worked, his long hours, and I remember thinking as a kid that I never wanted to go into that line of work. I've since changed my opinion about that, though. Working at Caroline's will give me the chance to sort of reconnect with my father—he died a few years back—and maybe it'll interest me enough to pursue the restaurant business like my dad did. Maybe, that is. Right now, I'm seeing the waiting job as a way to pay bills."

Getting the job as a waiter wasn't easy. With no professional experience working in a restaurant, he had to convince the management that he could handle the job and do it well. Although Caroline's wasn't the most expensive restaurant in town, it was one that offered a relatively sophisticated wine and beer list and menu. "I knew I would have to get the manager to see I was capable of handling myself at his restaurant," Carl said. "So I talked to a couple of the waiters and waitresses I had become friendly with over the years, and they told me what I needed to do. I then went to the bookstore to buy some books about the restaurant business and about wines. When I got to the check-out counter, I stopped myself when I pulled out my credit card from my wallet. 'Wait a minute, Carl,' I said to myself. 'You're using your credit card to buy books to help you get a job that's meant to pay off your credit-card debt. Get a grip.' So I went to my local library instead and checked out the very same books. After reading them, I called the restaurant manager and scheduled an interview. The next day he called me at my office and told me I got the job! I started work the following week."

Since he's been at Caroline's, Carl has significantly reduced his debt to the mid-three figure range. "I couldn't have gotten to that point without the new job. I'm still liking my job at the insurance company, especially as it gives me my health and medical benefits. This job has been terrific for me. Not only have I gotten to pay off almost all my debt—I'll be completely debt free in two months—I've gotten to spice up my life by meeting new friends and learning about a new business from the inside. But you know what the best thing about this job is? I'm sleeping a lot better at night."

◆ ◆ ◆

Investor Extraordinaire:
Wendy's Story

Numbers never appealed to Wendy, even in college. In fact, she spent the total of one day in her Introduction to Economics class in college before dropping it. "Sitting there watching the professor pointing to charts and diagrams on the blackboard, and listening to him talk on and on about supply and demand just wasn't for me," said the English major. "I remember sitting in class thinking, 'Wendy, your brain doesn't work like this. You'd better get out of here before you make even bigger mistakes come exam time.' So, I transferred out of economics and into a class on Middle English, which I loved and got an 'A' in."

Her English degree did her well. Today, Wendy is an English teacher in a middle school in Albuquerque, New Mexico. She also works part-time as a tutor. "I took the tutoring job initially to pay off my college and graduate school loans," said the twenty-eight-year-old. "I repaid the loans almost a year ago. The month after I paid them, I had a party for my friends, using the money that would have been my loan payment. It was a lot more fun giving the money to the caterers than to my bank.

"That was all nearly a year ago. The money I was making as a tutor, I was putting into a low-interest savings account at my local bank. I wasn't making any money off my money, if you know what I mean. I would keep reading the newspaper about the stock market breaking records and how it seemed everyone in the world, except me, was making money off Wall Street. I had no idea how to invest my money, or whom to call to invest it for me. Balancing my check book is a big deal to me, so finding someone to invest my money was beyond my imagination."

One Saturday morning, Wendy was reading her local newspaper when she saw an advertisement for a financial planning seminar that would be given that very night by an investment banker from a local securities firm. "What immediately attracted me to the ad was that it was aiming to attract new investors, people unsophisticated as to how the stock market works," said Wendy. "I've heard of the firm the broker works for, and I knew it to be reputable. So, I went to the seminar, which was held at our local YMCA, and I learned a great deal. I'll always be thankful I went. The best part of the program was that the banker gave us the information in an easy-to-understand format. If it wasn't over my head, then I know it wasn't over anybody else's head either." Wendy would later learn that similar seminars are offered around the country by different firms and agencies. "After I went to my seminar, I told some of my family and friends about it, and they told me how they've gone to similar seminars in their hometowns. They said they had told me about them, but I guess I just wasn't listening. Beside, I never had the money to invest until I repaid my loans."

She adds: "One of the investment strategies I learned about at the seminar was mutual funds. They're an easy and relatively safe way to invest in the market, and you don't have to be a millionaire to get involved in Wall

Street that way. The broker told us the names of some well-regarded mutual-fund companies and the interest rates a person can make off a fund that's doing well. Did you know that you can stand to make five times more money in a mutual fund than in a savings account? I didn't, until the seminar. The banker also told us what we needed to do to open a mutual fund, and about how we could go about doing so. Of course, one way was to rely on him and his firm. But, to tell the truth, the guy seemed honest and hard working, so I thought, 'Why not invest with him?' I called him a few days later, and ever since then I've been a player on Wall Street. I've actually gotten into watching how the Dow is doing. Who would have ever thought, me investing in the stock market?

"The easiest part of my investment is that the money is taken right out of my checking account each month by the mutual fund company. You complete a form that allows the fund to do this. Or you can mail in your investment on a monthly basis, but I find it easier and more efficient to have the company do it for me directly. I know that if I had to rely on myself to send in the money I would come up with every reason not to. This way, I know I'm making an investment each month. My broker—I love hearing myself say that, especially as I never thought I would ever have a broker—has projected how much money I'll have in my fund over different periods of time, say after five and ten years. I don't mind telling you I'll be somebody you're going to want to know. I'm not saying I'll be buying any mansions with my investment, but it will be a nice nest egg for my retirement."

❖ ❖ ❖

4

STRETCHING PART-TIME EMPLOYMENT INTO FULL-TIME

So you have a job that you enjoy, and you are interested in turning this part-time opportunity into full-time pay. Naturally, some jobs offer more leeway in securing a full-time position. For example, a small retail store may not yield much upward mobility; a larger corporation, however, may have multiple opportunities for promotion in a variety of departments. Before you consider such commitments, ask yourself these questions: Is this a field that I am interested in devoting my efforts to full-time? Is there an increase in benefits and pay equal to the increase in hours? Is the increase in pay worthwhile? Is this environment tolerable for more hours per day, or more days per week? Do I enjoy the company of my superiors and peers?

If you have answered the questions honestly and fully,

weighing the pros and cons, and decided to pursue full-time employment in your current position, there are many things you need to do to prepare. A career counselor in Washington, D.C. suggests: "Attempting to secure full-time employment from a current part-time position is a job in and of itself. If you haven't been a model employee, start immediately. Give yourself a few weeks to impress your boss and coworkers before you ask for that promotion. If you ask for this while you have mediocre skills and a nonimpressive reputation, chances are you will not get the job. Focusing on your job skills involves actively examining your behavior in a variety of domains, such as time management and rapport with your boss and co-workers. If you are pressed for time in terms of polishing your skills, focus primarily on the ones you are lacking."

Remember, too, that it is not quite enough in this case just to "do your job." You must go beyond the scope of your normal duties and be a highly visible contributor to the overall operation, so help out whenever you can. Never complain about these extra efforts; they will pay off in the long run. The worst thing that can happen is you will have a marvelous resource for referral and recommendation. Extra effort is never wasted. Remember, though, to stay within the realm of your job description and don't step on anyone's toes.

KEEP A JOB LOG

From the very first day that you are employed, take notes. You will want to refer to these notes to cite specific examples when it comes time for promotion.

Keep your notes together in a single notebook. On a

weekly basis, faithfully record a list of your positive contributions to your department. Your list should include your ideas, achievements, problem-solving solutions, coping skills, and cost-cutting suggestions and strategies, etc.

Look at your job description. Write down examples of how you have met or exceeded specific tasks. Make note of how you have saved the department money or time. Suggest ideas for future improvements, as creative solutions are especially welcomed. This is also a good place to keep samples or letters from other people who have benefited from your hard work.

Here is an excerpt from a job log of a person who holds a part-time job at a local social service agency. He writes:

Tuesday, August 13

Today I offered a solution to maximize administrative time efficiency. I suggested to my supervisor that a step be eliminated in terms of delivering time sheets to our downtown office. The current plan had one person filling in the time sheets and then giving them to another person to review and physically hand deliver. This had always been the way this task was performed. I simply suggested that the same person complete the time sheets and use the interoffice van, which makes deliveries every half hour, instead of giving them to another employee (who frankly hated this chore) to deliver. She now had more time to devote to her duties, and the van driver, who was still doing his job, was not overwhelmed by one more envelope. My boss wholeheartedly welcomed this alternate plan. He was quite impressed with my "innovative thinking." He said that the company had gotten used to a mode of thinking and sorely needed a fresh perspective.

Having a factual, complete journal enables you to present your supervisor with a comprehensive picture of your contributions to the company when you are requesting full-time employment. Often, employees forget about specific ideas and solutions they may have implemented. Write them down and review them often to remind yourself of incidents and suggestions. This is also a source of positive reinforcement for a job well done.

FEEDBACK

During your self-imposed probationary period, you should be receiving critical feedback from your supervisor, commending you on various efforts and suggesting improvements in other areas. Keep a list of both positive and negative comments in your job journal. If you haven't been receiving feedback, ask for it! Ask your supervisor about your strengths and weaknesses. Now you are able to take advantage of this feedback by actually applying suggestions and eliminating other behavior. You can also use this information to modify future applications. For example, if your boss compliments you on your phone skills or your knowledge of office machines, you can carry with you, and utilize, the knowledge that you are somehow exceptional in this regard. If your boss tells you that you aren't filing things properly, or that you never seem to be there when she needs you, you should note that as well. This is not a personal attack. It is useful information about how others view you on the job. Your ability to listen and actually apply feedback demonstrates to your employer that you are interested in learning how to improve your job performance and, in turn, enhance the company.

Now that you have recorded both feedback and positive contributions, you need to focus on improving your interpersonal skills. Stand out in the crowd early, so when you do begin pursuing a promotion, your boss will be familiar with your performance.

MAINTAIN A PROFESSIONAL RAPPORT WITH YOUR BOSS

Whether you're working to do well at your full-time or part-time job, maintaining a professional rapport with your boss is essential. For part-timers looking to stretch part-time work into a full-time position, however, it's especially important. Often, an office supervisor isn't going to assume that the part-time employee is seeking a full-time position at the firm. In addition, the part-time employee isn't part of the professional fabric of the office, so the supervisor might not scrutinize her work as closely has she might the work of a full-time employee.

Here's how you can impress your boss so that you can obtain the full-time position you're seeking:

Loyalty is one of the most important personal traits to practice at work. Your boss will notice that you are a faithful employee as opposed to having a reputation at work for badmouthing your supervisor. Even though it is common for many employees to make themselves feel superior by negatively attacking their boss, do not engage in this practice. Sometimes this is tempting, especially if it is warranted; however, this type of talk does not resolve the problem, and often your boss will find out. Lisa, an office manager, told a story where she joined a session to vent about problems at work, particularly about her boss. After she stated her mind by frankly griping about him, she found this information was personally reported to herboss an hour later by one of the people that had set up the session. Lisa wisely learned that she would never again criticize the job or other employers in public. Also note that gossip contributing to internal office politics is just as detrimental. Gossiping has a way of haunting you.

TIPS FOR SUCCESS

LEARN THE BOSS'S STYLE

Learn the manner in which your boss gets things done. In particular, learn to know her approach to problems, relationships with others, and her attitude toward the company.

Knowing her professional characteristics and expectations will help shape your own behavior. If you find your boss is a model employee, this will make your task easier. That is, by following her lead, you will find it easier to navigate the complexities of your office professionally. Yet, if your boss's style is to focus on the negative, accept the critical comments and couple it with positive information. For example, let's say your boss did not like the section of your presentation focusing on time management. She was harshly critical and tended to focus on that section only. However, when asked how the presentation was in general, her response was more positive and encouraging. By learning the manner in which your boss communicates, you can be better managed by your boss and emulate her positive attributes. You can also manage your boss by presenting the positive.

LISTEN TO YOUR BOSS

Take the time fully to comprehend what your boss is requesting of you and gear your actions to her requests. Following your boss's instructions, both carefully and completely, proves to your boss that you can process information and apply it in a concrete manner. It can be helpful also to listen to what your boss says to coworkers. When coworkers are praised or criticized you can apply this information to your own office behavior without suffering repercussions. Your boss will see that you are both insightful and show initiative.

WORK WELL WITH YOUR OFFICE PEERS

Maintain a cooperative, not competitive, relationship with coworkers. Often, there is hostility in the workplace, especially toward a new employee who is perceived as a threat. Do not contribute to this hostile situation by becoming aloof or isolative. Insure that your actions focus on teamwork and sharing information. Value your role as a team player. By establishing such a relationship, your peers can provide you with useful information about the work environment, such as that your boss will not tolerate lunch breaks that exceed 60 minutes, even by 20 seconds. This sharing of information between peers can help you to avoid pitfalls firsthand. It will also allow your coworkers to perceive you as a professional, yet sensitive, employee.

Keep a sense of humor at work. Humor is what can make you fit in with your coworkers and show others that some situations are not life and death. By laughing at your own mistakes, you can show others that you are human. While it is helpful to keep a sense of humor, you must remember that some humor is not tolerated in the workplace; make sure it is appropriate humor and never let it interfere with your work or your professional relationship with your boss.

Avoid profanity. This only serves to tarnish your professional image. You have other words in your vocabulary, so use them instead.

Now that you have polished your interpersonal skills, let's take a look at your job competence. Are you getting your job done in a manner that will catch your boss's eye when you ask for that promotion?

CREATE A POSITIVE FIRST IMPRESSION

Get acquainted both with your coworkers and your job. Meet a few people every day, instead of trying to remember a million names in one day. Don't let others think that you are a snob, even if you are just shy. Ask questions. Try to obtain information specifically regarding your position.

SET HIGH WORK STANDARDS FOR YOURSELF

High work standards begin by familiarizing yourself with your job requirements and supplies. Once you are familiar with these basics, you can maximize your time and money and your services, hence, increasing your productivity. Work fast while producing accurate, high-quality work. Dedication also compliments high work standards. Be willing to do more than is required. Prove to your boss that you show a sincere interest in the company's success. This may require that you come in early and stay late to get the job done. Show initiative. Once you are familiar with your boss's style and expectations, prove that you can do the right thing at the right time, without being told. Make creative suggestions. Volunteer for extra projects and committees to become noticed not only by your immediate supervisor, but also by others in the organization.

ASK QUESTIONS IF YOU ARE UNSURE

No one gets in trouble for asking questions, yet many people suffer the repercussions of keeping their mouth shut and guessing. A boss expects new employees to ask questions in order to obtain pertinent information about the company or position. Although it is expected that you ask questions, don't ask the same ones repeatedly. Write down your questions and the given answers, if necessary. If you feel uncomfortable asking too many questions, research answers. The training period is usually when most information concerning your position is presented. Ensure that your training is both comprehensive and relevant to aiding you in understanding what is required of you. Ultimately, you will be glad that you did ask questions, especially when it comes time to perform the once-confusing task.

ADMIT YOUR MISTAKES AND LEARN FROM THEM

Everyone makes mistakes on the job, especially when you're new. The important thing to remember is that there is something to be learned from your mistakes. Clarify exactly what your mistake entailed and get feedback about what can be done in future situations. Accept suggestions for improvement. Do not repeat your mistakes. Write them, and suggestions, down in your job log.

OBTAIN MORE EDUCATION OR TRAINING

One of the best ways to prepare yourself for a full-time

position is to take extra courses or training on your own time. Community colleges offer multiple job-related courses at night, when working people can attend. These include computer training, accounting, business administration, managerial skills, and a variety of specific technical training. Take multiple courses. Ask for advice from your boss regarding which programs could enhance your job performance. Not only will she provide you with helpful advice, your boss will undoubtedly be impressed by your eagerness to learn. Some organizations may offer some sort of financial assistance or reimbursement for education. When you've completed your course work, report your progress to your boss. Request that your grade or certificate be placed in your work file. This extra education provides a practical way to prepare for a full-time position or to move into a management position by mastering technology and keeping your skills up to date.

How are your time-management skills on the job? Is your work performance both accurate and efficient?

PRIORITIZE YOUR TASKS

Organize your time by determining what tasks are most important and need to be completed first. If you are uncertain, ask your boss which projects are most important. Do not procrastinate. If you are a morning person, focus on getting most work done during this time. By identifying your best time for working on difficult and important tasks, you are able to manage your time effectively. You can also maximize your time by working or learning during commuting hours.

If your time management skills are up to par, are you a dependable employee, in general?

ARRIVE TO WORK ON TIME

Tardiness in the workplace is unprofessional. It immediately tells your boss that you are not interested in committing to your job. If you are finding that it is difficult to arrive on time for work, mentally change the time that you need to arrive. Set your alarm ahead and come to work a half hour early. Not only will you be on time, your boss will now notice your enthusiasm. You will be able to prepare more effectively by organizing your daily schedule. This promptness does not only pertain to the early-morning hours. Remember always to arrive on time for meetings and appointments throughout your work day.

COMPLETE WORK ASSIGNMENTS ON TIME

It is extremely important to adhere to deadlines. By not completing tasks on time you are projecting incompetence and a lack of responsibility. If you are having difficulty completing tasks on time, reevaluate your time management techniques. Perhaps you are devoting too much time to other insignificant duties. Make sure that you have indeed prioritized your tasks correctly. If you are still having difficulty once you have personally reevaluated your techniques, ask a competent, well-respected coworker for advice on how to complete tasks on time. Experienced coworkers can share important information about how they work and prioritize their time and task management.

Now that we have examined work ethics and personal skills, it is essential to mention compatibility in the workplace. These social skills are just as important as interpersonal and competence skills. Having social deficits can prove to be just as detrimental in terms of procuring full-time employment.

LIMIT THE AMOUNT OF SOCIALIZING ON THE JOB

You are paid to do a specific job and not to chat with coworkers. People notice when you are devoting more time to hanging out at work than you are to your job. Excessive socializing will affect your overall job performance. Your work will be less polished, incomplete, or not turned in on time if you are spending too much time talking. Other coworkers may become annoyed by your incessant chatting. They will also become annoyed if your tasks are relegated to them because you are unable to complete your assignments on time. Save most of your socializing for lunch breaks or after work, not on the job.

PARTICIPATE IN SOCIAL ACTIVITIES

Participating in your company's social events is an effective way to get to know other employees and your supervisors. It is also a means of letting others to get to know you. By getting to know a wide variety of people in different departments, you are increasing your network pool. Bob in accounting can provide you with helpful information, just as Judy in human resources can. Get to know as many people as you can. Since social activities do have ulterior motives, maintain your professional demeanor when attending social functions. This does not mean that you have to be uptight. Remember that your actions and reputation are always on view, and just that because things are said or take place out of the office does not mean they will not come back to haunt you.

WEAR APPROPRIATE, PROFESSIONAL ATTIRE TO WORK

People are judged by how they look and how they dress. If you present yourself as a disheveled, coffee-stained employee in unpressed clothing, bosses usually infer that your work will also reflect your slovenly appearance. Moreover, wearing excessively tight or low cut clothing does not convey a professional image. Coordinate your wardrobe in terms of what your office dictates, and always keep your clothing clean, pressed, and in good repair.

Learning to see yourself as others see you is a skill worth learning. Here is an inventory to help you recognize areas you need to work on before you seek full-time employment. Focus your efforts accordingly.

EMPLOYEE SKILLS INVENTORY

Rating Scale:
5—Excellent   4—Good   3—Average
2—Needs Improvement   1—Poor

1. I have a professional rapport with my boss, practicing loyalty and relating to the boss's style. ____
2. I work well with my office peers, maintaining a cooperative attitude. ____
3. I created a positive first impression. ____
4. I have high work standards. ____
5. I often ask questions when I am unsure about assignments. ____
6. I am able to admit mistakes and to learn from them. ____

7. I am interested in my training and have made efforts to obtain more education. ____

8. I employ time management techniques and prioritize tasks. ____

9. I arrive to work and complete projects on time. ____

10. I am able to attend social activities and maintain a professional manner and limit on-the-job socializing. ____

Once you have improved your employee skills, it is time to focus actively on pursuing full-time employment. Your first step is to find what opportunities await you. There are five standard routes.

THE BULLETIN BOARD

Is there an up-to-date job board posting employment opportunities within your present workplace? Most organizations are obligated to post job listings within the organization before presenting them to outside sources. This enables current employees to move upward in the organization and, in turn, increases employee morale. It also saves the company time and money by not having to train someone from the outside. If your place of employment does not have a job board, there are other places to obtain such information.

THE BOSS

Your boss should tell you if there is an opportunity within your department. This is why maintaining a professional rapport with your boss is essential. Now you are able to come to your boss with concerns of your own and with concrete data to support your requests. Moreover, your boss may be able to tell you of opportunities in other departments, or make calls on your behalf to the human resources department.

If there is a specific department that you are interested in working, perhaps your boss knows someone and would be helpful in getting you reassigned. Set up a meeting to discuss this matter. Focus on the positive aspects of your job before you make requests. Starting off by complaining or focusing on problems will put your boss in a negative frame of mind.

Paige, a part-time mail room clerk, used this approach when she approached her boss: "Mr. Jones, I have enjoyed this past year working part-time in the mail room, and I have learned much about the company in this time. Now, I feel my skills could be best utilized by working as an assistant, especially in terms of the time-management and problem-solving strategies I utilize daily." She got the job. Be honest without overdoing it. Most bosses can tell when you are laying it on too thick. If there are specific reasons for your requesting full-time employment, now is the time to state them. If finances are your primary concern, indicate to your boss that an increase in hours would be an increase in pay without directly blaming your boss for not providing you with a raise. This is the time to review some of your contributions that you have carefully recorded in your job log. Point out to your boss how you have exceeded your job description, and how you would like the opportunity to do this on a full-time basis.

THE PERSONNEL OFFICE

If your boss cannot help, seek help from your human resources office. Tell your boss what you are planning to do, otherwise your boss may feel insulted that you are going behind her back. (You still need the boss's favorable recommendation.) Then make an appointment with the human resources director or manager. Don't waste valuable time by beginning with an interviewer. See if your boss can contact the personnel director personally to address your case.

Once you meet with the personnel director, be positive. This, again, is when you want to focus on your contributions to the corporation. Present the director with concrete examples from your job log. Explain how you have enjoyed your part-time position and working for the company overall. Emphasize how you want to explore all internal opportunities before you seek full-time opportunities elsewhere.

Undoubtedly, the personnel director will ask why you are seeking full-time employment. As was the case with your boss, present your position in a positive manner. Instead of complaining that your present position is a dead-end, suggest that your abilities would be best utilized in a full-time position in the accounting department because you are good with computation. Never mention that you are bored with your job. Instead, state that you have already excelled in your present part-time position. Don't mention money if you can avoid it. It is usually a given that an increase in hours and responsibility means an increase in pay. Avoid mentioning conflicts that you have with coworkers or your boss. This only serves to make you appear difficult to work with and that you are not a team player. This meeting with the human resources director is not the time or place for personal complaints or gripes. You are selling yourself based on your strengths; don't resort to weak tactics.

Ideally, the human resources director will aid you in locating full-time opportunities within the organization that suit your needs and requests. Sometimes you will be expected to meet multiple times to determine what is available specifically for you. If your company is rapidly growing, then your response should be quick; however, if there is not much opportunity, expect results to be somewhat slower. It is good to check back with human resources, but do not contact them on a daily basis. Constant pestering will most likely serve to impair your progress and not speed it along.

OTHER BOSSES

Given the proper approval (make sure *your* boss knows what you are up to), other management- and executive-level people in the company can be a great resource for finding full-time employment. Become friendly with these people's secretaries, and always be professional. You should make your inquiry in writing and set up a meeting with the executive to discuss your goals within the company. In meetings, be positive and stress how you are looking for advancement out of enthusiasm, not because you resent your present situation. Use your relationship with your own boss to enhance your relationship with the management of other departments. Make sure you know what the other departments do, and make sure that you have sketched out what your contribution to that department would be. People will ask you these questions. Make sure you have solid responses prepared. Treat this interview much as you did your talk with the human resources director, only remember that this boss does not need to go to work for you. It is the human resources director's job to help you. The boss of another department will only help you if she can gain from doing so.

THE GRAPEVINE

You can usually feel out the possibilities for other positions at the company through the office grapevine. You need to listen for opportunities and let others know that you'd like to work at the firm full-time. (Keep in mind the warnings above; just because you are not actively improving your job skills doesn't mean you can let them slide.) You can look around to gather information, too. This works both ways. You can keep your ears open for employment opportunities down the road and get a jump on them well before they are announced, and you can find out who is slated for what job and not waste your time pursuing it. You can ascertain who is getting ready to resign and jockey for her position. You can also reap information about the general rate of advancement and the level of increase in responsibility and pay you can expect. Pay attention to whether or not you are on track in the company—are you advancing at an average rate, being given the same opportunities as your coworkers, are you ahead of the curve, behind it? Stay aware of what is going on around you, and use what you find to your benefit.

A note about follow-up letters: It is a good idea, in general, to write follow-up letters to those who have interviewed you for job advancement. Such letters show appreciation and professionalism. They also serve to remind the recipient one more time of who you are. It is a general principle that people remember things best when they are told three times. Your inquiry was your first contact, your interview your second, and your follow-up letter your third. These letters should be short and to the point. Thank the person for seeing you, and say that you enjoyed the meeting very much. Also, say that you see possibilities for yourself in the company and look forward to hearing from or working with the person in the future. In your letter, restate your case, but don't be repetitive. State that you think you would be a fine addition to the team, that you see a place for yourself there. You should mail any correspondence within four days of your interview.

A note about temporary work: Temp work is a great way to get part-time work and to get to know businesses and companies. You can learn a lot about an industry by temping in it, without making the kind of commitment implicit in direct-hire work. It is a good way to fill in gaps in your own path, and often temp positions can turn into full-time employment. Temp agencies are well-prepared to find you work, and many firms approach them first to fill in for odd jobs. You should find which temp agencies are respected in your community and approach them. (You no doubt learned a great deal about temp agencies by reading the first chapter of this book.) You can also research the rate of permanent hire for these agencies. Talk to people who have used the agency and gather their impressions. Use the ideas sketched above to construct a comprehensive description of your skills before applying for a temporary position, and don't jump at the first one offered. You want to land a job that utilizes as much of your talent as possible. You will enjoy it more, and your chances for future employment will be greater. The agency will have its own rules and standards. Make sure you abide by these as you would any employer's. As always, keep your eyes and ears open. Temp work gets you in the door, staying there is your job.

◆ ◆ ◆

Volunteering: Jack's Story

Jack works in the library at a large metropolitan museum. Prior to gaining full-time employment there, Jack worked as a volunteer for six months in the gift shop. "I always wanted to work in an art museum," Jack explained. "I applied for jobs; the problem was I didn't have any experience. A woman in the human resources department suggested that I volunteer at the museum. Since employment wasn't feasible, I marched over to the volunteer office."

Volunteering is an excellent opportunity to scout out employment in a specific environment. Volunteering provides one with contacts in a variety of departments. "I wasn't really enthusiastic about volunteering in the gift shop, but this was a popular museum with many volunteers. I took any volunteer job I could get. Since the holiday season was approaching, the gift shop requested extra volunteers," stated Jack.

Volunteer opportunities need to be treated like a job; the same basic rules that govern a full-time job also apply.

"I knew from the first day that being late to work was a serious infraction. The manager of the gift shop told me of a recent volunteer that they had to let go because of chronic tardiness. Therefore, I made it a point to always leave for work in plenty of time to get there before I was expected. My supervisor noted that I was always early and often praised me for my dependability," Jack continued.

Feedback is also important when volunteering. If your supervisor does not readily give feedback, ask for it. Inquire about your strengths *and* weaknesses. Ask how you can improve your volunteer performance. "My supervisor always knew I was eager to work, but he was surprised when I asked for feedback. Initially, he did not have any negative feedback to give me. Then I told him I wanted to learn the qualities that were appreciated in an employee at the museum and how I could better myself. Once he understood that I was interested in permanent employment, he set up a time for supervision.

"During this meeting, my supervisor explained the qualities that were demanded of employees of the museum. Such qualities included dependability, loyalty, cooperation, creative problem-solving skills, and dedication. My supervisor also told me about training programs sponsored by the museum which volunteers were invited to attend. I jumped at the opportunity. At the training session, I learned about problems and other issues that various departments encounter in the museum. These seminars were both interesting and informative. I took notes. I learned people's names in different departments."

Another good way to meet people in various departments is to participate in social events hosted by the organization. Many companies sponsor parties, especially around the holiday season. When you attend these events, don't limit your socializing to the people in your department. Branch out. Introduce yourself to others. Inquire which departments people work for and find out roles of these departments. See which people are enthusiastic about their job and why. This is a great opportunity to acquire information about the organization; but remember, some people do attend social events to relax and to forget the mundane aspects of their jobs. If people do not readily offer information, don't press them. This will only make you look overly eager. Also remember, although alcohol is served at most employee functions, it is unprofessional to become inebriated.

"I went to the Christmas banquet hosted by the museum," said Jack. "It was a beautiful affair. Beside the free food, I obtained much free information. A garrulous coworker from the gift shop introduced me to many of her friends who worked throughout the museum. I made a point to talk with as many representatives from different areas of the museum. I hit it off with the people that worked in the art library. I could tell that they appreciated both working in the library and with each other. A few days later, they invited me to join them for lunch in the employee cafeteria."

The grapevine is a useful resource in searching for employment opportunities. Employees usually know about job openings before the general public does. Another solid resource is the job board. Most organizations advertise internally before placing an ad in the "help wanted" section of the paper. Utilize both resources on a regular basis. Opportunities do change daily.

"I started eating lunch with my friends from the library on a regular schedule," Jack continued. "But they knew I always checked the job board before I ventured into the cafeteria. My friends often teased me about my relentlessness about getting a job at the museum, but when a job became available in the library I was always the first person to know. I was soon introduced to the head librarian and discussed responsibilities regarding the circulation job. Because of my hard work and serious attitude regarding my volunteer job, my boss gave me a glowing recommendation. The day after I applied for the job, I was hired. A few months of volunteering provided me with the opportunity that I always wanted. But it was not just the volunteering. It was the respect that I showed to my supervisor, the other employees of the museum, and to the work itself."

◆ ◆ ◆

Eagerness Is Key:
Sara's Story

Sara is a recreational therapist in a psychiatric ward at a local hospital. She worked part-time for only two months before she was offered full-time employment with benefits. "Eagerness," said Sara, "is the secret to obtaining a full-time job. Let your boss know from day one that you are interested in a full-time position."

Sara had asked many general questions during her initial interview for the job. "I wanted to know basically what the job required of me and with what type of person they were seeking to fill the position. By obtaining this information during the interview, I was able to present the qualities they endorsed on the very first day of the job."

Other benefits of getting the basic facts during the interview is that one can focus on more detailed attention to questions that specifically pertain to the job. Sara was able to ask detailed questions about what her daily schedule would be like. Sara recorded both her questions and her supervisor's answers in a notebook.

"I found this system very useful," contended Sara. "Whenever I was uncertain about a procedure, or my boss provided me with pertinent information about my responsibilities, I recorded it in my job log. It's extremely difficult to remember all the information that is presented to you during the first few days on the job. By writing everything down in my job log, I was able to use this as a reference guide. The most embarrassing thing to happen during the first days on the job is to do something the wrong way because of information overload. It's unprofessional for your boss to have to repeatedly correct you, despite the fact that you have asked the right questions. If you don't understand, ask, but use the information given: don't merely forget it."

Sara also suggested other good things to include in her job log:

- all feedback, the positive and the negative
- names and titles of coworkers
- daily schedules
- where things are located in the building
- ideas and suggestions for improvements to be made in her department
- why tasks are performed certain ways
- important phone numbers

After the first week of orientation and diligent recording in her job log, Sara had a firm grasp of what the job entailed. "Equipped with a greater knowledge of the job, I was now able to focus on how to perform my job well. I knew what was required of me based on the job description, but I wanted to exceed those expectations."

However, before you exceed any expectations, Sara reminds us, you have to make sure that you cover the basic rules of being a good employee:

1. arrive to work on time, but a little early can't hurt
2. establish a professional relationship with both your boss and coworkers
3. complete work assignments on time
4. listen carefully to feedback
5. learn from your mistakes
6. don't complain, gossip, or curse

Perhaps the most important rule to focus on is developing a good rapport with both your boss and coworkers.

First, your boss: Listen to what your boss says. Watch how she works. "When I first started my job as a recreational therapist, I asked my boss if I could sit in on one of her groups that she held with the patients," Sara continued. "I wanted to see, specifically, how she structured her time during the activity, and how she responded to patients. My boss thought it was a great idea. I eventually sat in on multiple groups and learned a great deal from my boss. Afterward, I was able to ask her why she responded in certain ways and what she thought was beneficial in her group. I learned much by watching and listening. I was able to incorporate the ideals that my boss stressed in my own groups."

Honing in on your listening and observational skills with your boss is very important, but many things can be learned through coworkers. "From the beginning, I enjoyed the company of my coworkers. I also sat in on some of their groups and watched how they interacted with patients. I often asked their opinion and always asked questions if unsure of how to do something. I became close with my peers, especially since we shared the same office space. The only problem this posed was the easy accessibility to socializing. Because we were so close personally, it was easy to chat instead of writing the dreaded progress notes. I learned to prioritize my tasks. Together we decided to limit socializing to our hour-long lunch break.

"I also discovered that I was most productive after lunch, and so this was the time that I allotted to doing paperwork. I was fortunate enough to come into a working environment that espoused teamwork. The teamwork mentality was reinforced by covering others' groups when one went on vacation. I was always eager to help others. Covering others' groups also helped me gain a sense of the different populations in the hospital. Not only was I being a team player, I was learning more information about my job," Sara concluded.

Obtaining extra training or schooling always enhances your chance for promotion or full-time employment. This can be achieved by taking classes at local universities that pertain to your job modality or going to in-service courses. Said Sara, "I have always been a person that was interested in learning more. After the first two weeks at work, I asked my boss what type of classes I should take that would improve my job performance. She suggested a series of in-service courses. Moreover, she encouraged me to visit our out-patient department to see how the groups are structured there. I loved both. It was so informative to see the different focuses in the out-patient department and to appreciate their group techniques. My boss appreciated my zeal to learn."

Sara would later realize that the skills she utilized to get the full-time position would also work to her advantage as a full-time employee at the hospital.

"After the first month and a half that I was working part-time, a coworker approached me with her impending resignation," she said. "She had decided to pursue schooling full-time, yet because of our good relationship, she wanted me to know that she was leaving before she told my boss. This gave me a great advantage. In the two weeks before she gave her notice, I was able to receive pertinent feedback from my boss. I asked specifically about my strengths and weaknesses. My boss was very pleased with my performance, but she did offer some good suggestions for improvement. I was able to apply these techniques before my coworker turned in her resignation. My boss understood that I appreciated both my job and my responsibilities. The good news is I was offered the full-time position soon thereafter."

CONCLUSION

The world of part-time work is full of rewards and challenges. With the information and advice contained in *Moonlighting for Fun and Profit*, you now have the skills to find your ideal second job and to lead a happy and satisfying life once you've taken on part-time work. Perhaps the most important lesson you should take away from our book is that the key to success in any job—whether it's a full-time position or a part-time one—is organization. But organization for the person with a second job is especially important because of her added responsibilities and limited free time. Also, keep a record or journal handy through all phases of your job hunt. You'll also want to keep one handy once you've obtained the second job. You'll find that writing down your thoughts and professional experiences will help you be an even better qualified job applicant and employee. Now that you've mastered the ideas and information in *Moonlighting for Fun and Profit*, you are ready to reap the rewards of part-time employment.

INDEX